LEAP OF FAITH
God Must Be A Packer Fan

by

Steve Rose

John 3:3

Angel Press of WI   Wautoma, Wisconsin

1996

Angel Press of WI
PO Box 48
Neshkoro, WI 54960

Angel Press of WI
PO Box 48
Neshkoro, WI 54960

First Printing September 1996

Front cover photograph courtesy of
Robert Brooks and Professional Management, Inc.

Photos courtesy of the Green Bay Packers
unless credited otherwise.

Publisher.......................................Joseph H. Schlaefer
Editor...Larry Names

Table of Contents

To my best friend, my world, my angel, my wife,

Kim

Besides my Salvation in Christ,
you're the greatest gift God has ever given me.
Thanks for holding me during the storms on the long,
trying journey from the land of fears and tears
to our place, today, of happiness and joy.
You're the only one in the world
who would have gone through so much for me.
Thank you.
You're incredible.
Here's to a million more laughs—together.
I love you.

Steve Rose

ℱoreword

From the day I called Steve Rose from Phoenix, and he told me he was writing this book, I knew it was going to be *real* big. I've virtually seen this book's success already! It will be a success *not* because it's about the Green Bay Packers, but because it shows what happens when God chooses to use a group of people for His purposes.

This message needed to be told. Let me assure you that if this book were an arrow, it would hit the bull's-eye. The vision and information given in it is dead on!

Actually, it doesn't take a lot of faith to believe that God is the true leader of the Packers, which is just one of the issues in this book. Let me take you back a couple of years to tease and jog your memory.

Did you notice the change that came to Green Bay right after we signed Reggie White? Besides bringing a great game of football to town, what else is his mission? Who is his leader? What really makes him tick and gives him his purpose? His faith in the Lord, right? Doesn't it make sense miracles would follow him here?

I'll share with you that shortly after Reggie arrived in Green Bay he and Ken Ruettgers started an Accountability Bible Study Group on our team. Together, we sought God's will for the guys and our own lives. I agree with Ken Ruettgers when he said, "The miracles and other special things that have happened for the Packers are byproducts of the faith of the players and the fans."

So after talking with Steve, and I realized he was in Oshkosh writing this book, while and I was in Phoenix writing a song about many of the same things, it became clear we had work to do together. After you read this and hear the lyrics to my song, you will know exactly what I mean. We've said many of the same things about the love on this team for the community, and the fact that Packer fans are the greatest in the world.

Like many of you, I believe that the best is yet to come for the Green

Bay Packers.

You'll read exactly how I felt before the 1995 season and what happened during the year. I felt great things were on the way, and I still do! What do you think? Did big things happen last season, or what?

Most of it, and especially before last year's Monday Night Game with the Bears, I felt like nobody could cover me! That's the night Brett threw the 99-yard touchdown pass to me.

I believe this book is just a beginning. God bless you as you read it, and watch us as we tackle the 1996 season and win Super Bowl XXXI!

— Robert Brooks
#87

LEAP OF FAITH

God Must Be A Packer Fan

Author STEVE ROSE (right) and radio co-host KEN RUETTGERS in the hall of radio station WORQ in Green Bay.

$\boxed{I}$ntroduction

The Farm Boy Meets the Football Player

$\boxed{L}$ ike still, thick, humid air warning that a storm is on the way, Ken Ruettgers, Robert Brooks, and their teammates had prepared me that something big was going to happen with the Green Bay Packers. I first felt it in 1994 from my unique vantage point at WORQ Radio in Green Bay. It started as a spark and erupted into a flame, and it was all ignited back in July of the same year through a phone call.

"Hello, Roses," I answered.

"Steve, Chuck Towns from Q-90."

"Chuck, how are you?"

"Great," he said.

Chuck, the general manager of the non-profit listener supported Christian station in Packerland, had long been a friend in the radio business. Over lunch a couple months earlier, I'd told him I was taking a break between radio commitments.

"Hey, I'm in a real bind up here. I need somebody temporarily to do the morning show," explained Towns.

"How about me?" I inquired.

"That's why I'm calling!"

I decided to help. Along with doing the morning show, I was given the privilege of co-hosting a weekly radio talk show with Packer Ken Ruettgers called "Timeout". Because of Ken's Christian faith, he was a natural for the station, and I was called on to be the glue to pull it all together. On September 27, 1994, I officially entered into this ministry with Ken and the Green Bay Packers.

Until the morning I met Ruettgers, all I knew about him was that he was the Packers' number one draft pick in 1985 and had been their starting left tackle ever since. From his public service announcements on TV, I gathered that he was very family, cause, and community oriented. I also knew he liked Rush Limbaugh and that he was big—real big!

The September morning we met my suspicion about Ken's size was the first thing confirmed. Out of the corner of my eye, I saw a huge figure lumbering past the radio studio window in the hall. The shadow took a hard right and entered the control room where I was standing.

What a sight to behold! Picture Gentle Ben in a pair of tan shorts, wearing a XXXL white T-shirt. His arms and chest were bigger than a bear's, and thank goodness he was more polite than one. He walked slowly towards me looking directly into my eyes. He stuck out his bandaged, wounded right paw, and in a confident voice said, "Hi, Ken Ruettgers."

I looked way up into the eyes of the 6'6", 292-pound Packer veteran like a kid who had just met the President. But this wasn't the President; it was someone *more* important—a Green Bay Packer!

"Great to see you. I'm Steve Rose."

After a little small-talk, I handed him a list filled with some suggestions about what we could talk about during the show. I stammered, "Maybe after we rehash the game, we could chat about a few of these topics," I said.

"Sounds good," he said quickly, looking at the list.

Right then, I knew Ken wasn't going to be a very tough person to work with. I was right.

Ruettgers lowered his tired, sore body onto the soft, cushioned studio chair next to his microphone in Studio A. With my heart racing in the presence of a real Green Bay Packer, I coolly attempted to drum up some more conversation. I could hardly think straight, much less talk, but I tried.

"Wh-what happened to your hand?"

"I don't know. Musta got stepped on or something," he smiled.

With our relationship five minutes old, Ruettgers staggered me with a question that put me at great ease with him.

"What do you want me to bring you to drink each Tuesday morning?" he asked.

I was stunned! Why was he asking what he could do for me? I thought.

Very delighted and flattered I responded, "Some decaffeinated coffee with cream, if you really want to bring me something. That would be great. I can't have regular coffee. If I have the real stuff, I'll do somersaults around the studio during the show."

Ken laughed.

Somehow, my nerves survived our first show. Even though I'd been doing talk radio for years, I was intimidated by my new friend. Ironically, there are very few people on earth today that make me feel as comfortable as Ken Ruettgers.

Like peanut butter and jelly, Ruettgers and I have blended on the air, and all along I sensed that something was up with the Green Bay Packers, but what?

So it's been a memorable two years making the trips to Green Bay during the season for the show, while still taking care of my day-to-day duties with the VCY America Network in Oshkosh.

As the Packers wrapped up their third straight playoff berth and Packermania was entering a new realm, on December 22, 1995, just like two years ago, my phone rang. It was a phone call that has changed my life forever.

"Hi, this is Steve," I answered.

"Steve, this is Jim Zielinski."

Jim has long been my radio idol and good friend. He'd given me my first job in radio at WFON in Fond du Lac in 1979. Today, he's a marketing genius in Chicago. He was calling to share an idea he thought I should consider.

"Steve, you know what you should do? Why don't you write a book about your experiences with the Packers through your show with Ken? You're right in the middle of it. You can tell something is happening up there with the Packers, man!"

Zielinski had spent thirty years up in the Fox Cities, so he knew of Packermania firsthand.

"Jim, you're right. You and I know it's always been great to be a

Packer fan, but this year it's really gone to another level!"

"I know. You can see it from here in Chicago."

Time stood still as Zielinski kept talking and I started daydreaming. A vision of a picture of Robert Brooks leaping into the Green Bay crowd enveloped my mind. I could hear dialogue from the many Packer interviews I'd done with Ken, reminding me of great quotes like, "This is a great team, nobody cares who gets the credit, we think we can win it all!"

"Yeah, I'll give it some thought," I told my mentor regarding his tip for me to write a book. "I'll be in touch," I assured him.

Right after we hung up, I started to pray God would guide me as to whether this was part of His will for my life to do this. I asked the Lord to give me three confirmations in my heart if it was.

All day, I thought to myself, "Reggie's injury miracles over the last two years, the bonding, the camaraderie on the team, God's hand is in this! Should I tell the story?"

The next day, December 23, I began my Christmas shopping. I usually wait 'til Christmas Eve, but for some reason I started a day early. As I walked through the aisles of Shopko, in living color, the image "God Must Be A Packer Fan," shot to the forefront of my mind. *Sign one.*

On Sunday, Yancy Thigpen of the Steelers, provided the Packers with "the gift," the dropped pass that catapulted the Packers to the NFC Central Division title. I watched the replay of Thigpen as the game winning touchdown pass slithered through his fingers and bounced off his knee. I said to myself, "God *must* be a Packer fan! *Sign two!* One more and it's a go," I told myself.

By an opening playoff win against the Atlanta Falcons in Green Bay, the Packers earned a date with the San Francisco 49ers. It was slated for 3:00 p.m. Central time from the city of the Golden Gate Bridge.

Just before kickoff, I prayed, "God, I've tried to manipulate You enough over the years, and I don't want to tell You what to do. I only ask that Your will be done. But, God, a win over the 49ers would really let me know you want me to write this book!"

As Peter King, the lead NFL sportswriter from *Sports Illustrated* would tell me, "Ten minutes into the game you knew the 49ers couldn't win." Three hours later the Packers won. *Sign three!* My prayer and those of a few hundred thousand other Packer nuts had been fulfilled, and now it was time for me to hold up my end of the bargain. God had made Himself perfectly clear. I started writing.

The miracles, magic, and "God-incidences" haven't ceased here in Packerland. As of late, it's been a real challenge keeping up with the moves of God. Trying to squeeze them all into this book before the deadline was like running breathlessly to sneak onto an elevator as the door closed.

So welcome to my miracle. To Chuck Towns, Jim Zielinski, and most of all the Lord—thanks for calling.

And to you, my friends, I appreciate you for taking the leap of faith to read this book. Press on, and you too may come to believe that God *must* be a Packer fan!

STEVE ROSE (right) and KEN RUETTGERS in the studio at WORQ.

REGGIE WHITE is known as the "Minister of Defense" throughout the NFL because he is an ordained minister and he is considered to be one of the greatest defensive linemen to ever play the game.

One

The Leader of the Pack

Never one to duck his faith with anybody—including the press—Reggie White, the great defensive lineman, professed, "God healed me again. I know some of you guys don't want to hear that, but He did."

What made this announcement so stunning was Packer medical personnel had just two days earlier declared White through for the season because of a hamstring injury. White had suffered the serious injury against the Cincinnati Bengals in Green Bay on December 3.

Team doctors, medical personnel, and Reggie himself, all agreed to schedule surgery to repair the injury. The consensus was surgery would give him the best opportunity to return at full strength for the 1996 Packer campaign.

The news was so dramatic that a foam cheesehead hat could have dropped in Green Bay and it would have been heard all across Wisconsin and the Upper Peninsula of Michigan. It tugged at the hearts of all Packer fans. They were filled with dismay when they learned of the loss of their leader.

White provides spiritual guidance as well as serving as the overall team leader. He is the most well known and respected Christian on the Packers, in the National Football League, and arguably in all of professional sports.

Reggie was devastated. Having never won a Super Bowl, he knew this 1995 Green Bay Packer squad had a great chance of making it to the game pro football players dream of. It appeared all hope was lost. In nearby Appleton, the *Post-Crescent* cried:

NO MIRACLE FOR REGGIE THIS TIME

That newspaper and I, as well as many others, underestimated the power of prayer. "Just like my elbow injury last year, I didn't pray that God would heal me, but that His will would be done," said White, recalling how he'd recovered miraculously the year before to play in a Thanksgiving Day bash in Dallas. Now, a year later, God did it again. Here's how it happened.

White was home in the early evening rough-housing with his kids on the living room floor when he noticed an improvement in the condition of his hamstring. White called Kent Johnston, the Packer strength and conditioning coach. Johnston met White at the Don Hutson Center, the Green Bay Packer indoor practice facility. After a series of physical, mobility, and strength tests, Johnston astonishingly concluded that, in fact, Reggie's injury had drastically improved from just hours before. Fired with hope and the Christmas spirit of a child, White drove out into the holiday season night. He was off to bring glad tidings of joy to head coach Mike Holmgren. Even St. Nick couldn't deliver the present the "Minister of Defense" was about to lay under the coach's tree.

When Reggie arrived at Holmgren's home, the Packer head coach was just then coming outside to turn off the outdoor Christmas lights. Suddenly, he found himself face to face with his star player.

"Coach, with what I got to tell you, you just might think I am Santa Claus!" Reggie said.

Holmgren recounted later that he "thought (White) was Santa Claus."

Never one to doubt Reggie White's faith, Holmgren was, however, a bit skeptical. He wanted to get the word from the doctors himself.

Sure enough, the surgery was postponed, and White began to prepare for the upcoming game against the Saints. The miracle man, the guy who has always talked about the healing power of this Lord of his, indeed was ready to play again! Thousands of people all over the country were thanking and praising God with him.

Matt LaBounty, a second year Packer defensive lineman, was to fill in for White if Reggie couldn't play. After hearing of White's latest inexplicable medical phenomenon, LaBounty said, "If he's healed, I'm gonna start reading the Bible."

LaBounty's not alone. These mysterious miracles have whet the spiritual appetites of many who may have doubted the power of prayer and healing.

This may come as news to some, but White's elbow and hamstring miracles were not the only medical phenomena as of late on the Packers.

In the August pre-season finale against the Redskins in Green Bay, Ken Ruettgers, Packer offensive lineman, found himself lying in a heap of pain on the warm tundra of Lambeau Field. Packer head trainer Pepper Burruss confirmed that never in his 20 years in the National Football League had he seen anyone come back from as severe a back injury as Ruettgers did in such a short time. Although Ken was out two weeks, he missed just one game. From eight weeks to two, would you agree God was at work here also? Like Reggie, Ken's sudden medical improvement was simply amazing.

In the middle of the same season, Packer star quarterback Brett Favre suffered a severe ankle sprain in the Metrodome at Minneapolis during the Viking game. He could hardly walk the day after the injury. The Packers lost the game, but the thought of losing their quarterback for an undetermined amount of time hurt worse. With the spirit of divine healing on a rampage throughout the Packer locker room, the Packer hero kept his heart and mind open to Reggie's source of help, including God Almighty Himself. Days after his injury, Brett revealed, "Hey, I'm not as spiritual a person as Reggie, but the big man asked if he could put some oil on my forehead and pray for me. I said sure."

The following week Brett Favre not only played in a crucial game, but he probably had the greatest game of his life. In a see-saw affair, the Packers outlasted the Bears in front of a packed Lambeau house, 35-28. The media began to shout, "Brett Favre for M.V.P." Of course, this is the highest honor for a professional football player, being named the NFL's Most Valuable Player. To the delight of the fans, the boy from Kiln, Mississippi, easily won the *Most Valuable Player* award after the season. It was just the beginning of many accolades for the handsome, young quarterback for the 1995 season.

Reggie White's faith continued to rub off on Green Bay Packer fans and was having a positive impact everywhere. During a Packer playoff game against the Atlanta Falcons, the faithful called for his and the

Lord's help.

With second year guard Aaron Taylor lying on the grass of Lambeau field with a painful knee injury, Reggie White walked across the Lambeau turf to check on his wounded teammate. The fans began to yell things like, "Reggie heal him. Reggie, lay hands on him!" They weren't being sarcastic. Many truly felt and believed that the God who'd healed White from his injuries could help Aaron Taylor also.

Was it coincidence or "God-incidence" that both Reggie White and Ken Ruettgers were miraculously healed? Do the prayers of the players and fans count? Was something bigger than Bob Harlan, Ron Wolf, Mike Holmgren, Reggie White, and Brett Favre was—and is—guiding this team?

By the end of 1995, for the third straight year, the Packers were courting playoff possibilities. This along with the miraculous healings coupled with the immense player-fan bonding left Packer fans everywhere renewed.

If you still weren't convinced the Packers were the benefactors of divine intervention, all you had to do was watch the last 20 seconds of their regular season finale with the Steelers on Christmas Eve in Green Bay.

With the Central Division Title and Packer playoff possibilities on the line, Pittsburgh quarterback Neil O'Donnell marched the enemy Steelers down the field and into scoring range. On fourth down from the Packer 16-yard line, Yancy Thigpen, a Pro Bowl receiver, dropped a sure touchdown pass from O'Donnell in the end zone. As the ball fell from Thigpen's fingers, it propelled the Packer side of the teeter-totter skyward.

Gene Lefeber will never forget what he saw during that precious moment. "I was on my way to an office in the stadium when I heard the fans just roaring. I peeked out onto the field and saw Reggie White draped in a fan's banner taking a victory lap around the perimeter of the field saluting the fans. I've never ever had a feeling like that before. It sure fit on Christmas Eve."

The true impact of that one dropped pass cannot be really appreciated until you consider how the Packer season and team history would have been completely different if Thigpen had made that catch.

First of all, the win brought the Packers their first Central Division title in 23 years. The burden that had weighed heavily over the years on the team and coaches and management was now gone.

Second, the Packers hosted a playoff game with the Falcons in Lambeau Field, instead of going to Philadelphia. (The Eagles trounced the "hot" Detroit Lions that week. Could it have happened to the Packers instead of the Lions?)

Third, the complexion of the entire NFC playoff bracket picture changed. As we know, it worked out well, except for the NFC Championship which the Packers lost to the Cowboys, 38-27.

After the "gift" from the Pittsburgh Steelers, the press asked Reggie if God had knocked the ball out of Thigpen's hands. The tired lineman smiled, "I ain't gonna say that. I won't lay that on God!" The usually serious press corps roared with appreciation for his wisdom. White admitted the thought had crossed his mind.

The following week, the first of the playoffs, the Packers beat Atlanta, 37-20, before a soldout Lambeau Field crowd. The fans refused to leave after the game.

Coach Mike Holmgren walked off the field drenched with Gatorade. He peered over at *Sports Illustrated*'s Peter King and said, "This is why we do this."

Then the "angel-possessed" Packers left the hearts of 49er fans in San Francisco, slamming the door on Frisco's dream of back-to-back Super Bowl titles. Minutes into that game you knew the Packers couldn't lose. Like Rice-a-Roni, the green-and-gold gave their faithful fans a San Francisco treat—one that will live for some time in Green Bay memories.

However, where heaven resides, sometimes the forces of the enemy love to crash the party of the saints. Near the end of the 1995 Playoffs, Reggie White's Inner City Church in Tennessee was burned to the ground, allegedly by racial hatemongers. We wonder why things like this happen.

White, extremely hurt, dejected, and loaded with righteous anger, unwaveringly professed, "Every time Satan is a part of something like this, it usually means that God is up to something big."

Let's make one thing clear, Satan doesn't burn down churches; people do. But where Satan's rules are in force and he has his foot in the hearts and minds of the wicked, the Lord always has a response.

White turned out to be a prophet as fans came to the aid of their wounded hero. Selflessly they gave to the need of his church. The spirit of giving spread throughout the country. Donations, cards, letters, and other avenues of love and support from Wisconsin flooded Knoxville, Tennessee. The Packer family rallied to the cause and dove in, hearts first, to help.

As always, Reggie White made no attempt to hide his love for the people of Wisconsin who have embraced him. During the Pro Bowl in Hawaii, the beloved ordained minister told an NBC television audience, "I want the people in Green Bay to know that I care for them as much as they care for me." White was moved by the outpouring of love, especially in Wisconsin. While in Green Bay to accept funds to rebuild the church, White said, "You'll have to be patient with me for a minute. You might see a big man cry right here." Tearfully, he accepted the check for $143,261.42!

Just weeks later, the Whites accepted another gift of $95,000 raised in Milwaukee. The people at WPKR Radio in Oshkosh, Wisconsin, chipped in with $11,000 they had raised in a special promotion. Other gifts of love were still coming in.

The outpouring of love and unity that results from many tragedies, like this one, shows once again that when spider webs unite, they can tie up a lion. That when it's dark enough you can see the stars.

The law of sowing and reaping was at work in a way beyond expression. In this case fans planted seeds of love, and White, who had planted his own that fans have harvested, was now reaping a bountiful crop of love of his own for his ministry. He, in turn, will return it to the fields of Green Bay once more.

The church tragedy was not the only one that touched Green Bay. On January 14, 1996, the Green Bay Packers lost to the Dallas Cowboys—again. This time for the National Football Conference Championship. The fans have had to be patient and one more year before a Super Bowl victory is okay. Only Packer fans will persevere this long.

Someone once said, "Not everybody can be in the parade. Somebody needs to be sitting on the curb to wave as it goes by." The Green Bay Packers are the parade, the love-blind fans sit on the curb of the stands of Lambeau Field and wave. Evidence shows God is the One who has assembled the parade, and the loving bystanders. It's a divine union of people, and it's no secret.

"In my 12 years of covering the NFL, I have never seen a bonding between players and fans like I saw during the 1995 season in Green Bay," said *Sports Illustrated*'s Peter King. "There was an incredible development of a 'Mutual Admiration Society' between the players and fans. The fans were and are such a factor for the Packers. What's especially amazing is that Packer fans are like that regardless of the Packers' record."

Even the Milwaukee Brewers baseball team tipped their hats to Packers with a special invitation to two Packer players. On April 9, 1996, opening day for the Brewers, Robert Brooks and LeRoy Butler, who led the force of Packers known to jump into the stands after touchdowns, were invited to throw out the ceremonial first pitch.

It's unanimous in Wisconsin. As Steve Haas, sportswriter for the *Oshkosh Daily Northwestern*, put it, the atmosphere of Packer games in Green Bay has the feel of a "religious experience linked with a social bonding event." It is all part of the redundant football ambiance only found at Lambeau Field.

Some might push for the separation of God and athletics, eliminate post-game prayer, do away with celebrations in the end zone after scoring, and put an end to the "John 3:16 signs" that peek out between the goal posts during extra point kicks. Keeping that in mind, we ask you to ponder this. Where is the only football stadium on the face of the earth where 60,000 fans would stand up and cheer at the playing of *Amazing Grace? Amazing Grace,* not *Rock 'n' Roll Is Here To Stay*! I'll tell you where; Lambeau Field in Green Bay, Wisconsin!

During the 1995 season, Reggie White was being shown on the Jumbotron screen singing this hymn of praise to the Lord. (ESPN also played it before their Packer-Tampa Bay broadcast.) About halfway through the video, fans began to stand to honor and revere the Lord. As it ended, they chanted: "Reggie! Reggie! Reggie!," oblivious to the play down on the field.

It pumped up more than just the fans.

"I would have loved it if they would have played it when the defense was on the field 'cause it got so loud," said Ken Ruettgers. "It was great, as a Christian, listening to the crowd honoring God."

Robert Brooks said, "When they played that video, I got pumped!"

When the Lord speaks in Green Bay, through Reggie White and others, people listen!

ROBERT BROOKS has popularized Packer players leaping into the stands at Lambeau Field after they score a touchdown.

ᴛᴡᴏ

The Leaper of the Pack

T he media know-it-alls predicted the Packers would finish near the bottom of the Central Division in 1995. Robert Brooks, the man who epitomizes the Green Bay Packers, knew beyond a shadow of a doubt that they were wrong.

"I had a vision," he said, "before the season that we were going to have a great year and something special was in store for the team, the fans, and myself."

Those powerful words of faithful prophecy came to fruition, but how? Many were baffled by what happened in Green Bay in 1995.

Sports Illustrated's Peter King watched something virtually unexplainable happen during the season in Green Bay. "If someone would have told me a year ago that the Green Bay Packers would be a better team without Sterling Sharpe, I would have told you, 'You're crazy.' The fact is, they were, and they are," he confessed.

King believes the Packers did a heart and gut check after the media projections. "You can't measure or underestimate the edge that the media can provide to a team by declaring it nearly dead. The Packers, before the 1995 season, were labeled as a fourth or fifth place team. They didn't believe it. Neither did their fans."

Two cases in point:

Gene Lefeber from *America's Pack*, the official fan club of the Green Bay Packers, said, "When the articles started coming out with the pre-season predictions projecting the Packers finishing third in the Central Division, the first ones not to believe it were the fans. It was as if they called a meeting of the heart and said, 'We won't let this happen.' When the body of a family unites, it becomes a powerful force of faith." This appears to have been this first leap of faith of the '95 campaign.

Then well known Packer historian Larry Names voiced a contrary opinion to the media experts. In August, as a guest on Paul Kasperczak's *Coach's Corner* show on station WFCL in Clintonville, Wisconsin, Names told a northeast Wisconsin radio audience that "the magazine writers are wrong. The Packers are the team to beat in the NFC Central. In fact, the only teams capable of keeping them from the Super Bowl are the 49ers and the Cowboys. Barring a barrage of injuries to several key people at the same time, the Packers are a better team without Sterling Sharpe. This team is a team of destiny, if you will. Considering what happened with Reggie White last year with his elbow and all, I'd even go so far to say that this is a team that is divinely inspired."

A second leap in the right direction.

As for Robert Brooks, he wouldn't tolerate any thought that the Packers couldn't be as good a team with him replacing the injury fallen Sterling Sharpe. Brooks, who also performed under Sharpe's shadow at the University of South Carolina, found himself faced with trying to live up to "Sharpe" expectations in Green Bay. He read the papers. So did other Packers. He joined Brett Favre and Reggie White in leading the team into the 1995 season. Then, under Coach Holmgren's direction they proceeded to blow those expert opinions right out of the water.

And how did Brooks know this was all going to happen? Had he been given a glimpse of the future? One word is all that's necessary to answer this question. This five-letter word has been a force in building the foundation for his family ever since he was a little boy in South Carolina.

"My mom always said, 'You gotta have faith.' Even when you can't see it, you have to believe," said Brooks of this special woman in his life. No one knew more than he did the big shoes that needed to be filled with the loss of Sharpe. So when did Robert begin to see it happen?

"It was the Monday night game in Chicago. I just felt in my spirit that something big was on the horizon."

That night, September 11, the second game of the season, the Packers fought off the Bears in the nationally televised event to hang on for a 27-24 win. Had the Packers lost, it would have been their second in a row, putting them behind the proverbial eight ball early in the season.

A major part of the Pack coming up big was Brooks scoring on a 99-yard touchdown strike from Brett Favre, a Packer record.

Brooks appeared on the "Timeout" program with Ken Ruettgers and me on New Year's Day, 1996. It was a night I'll never forget, especially now as I look back and realize that only a few weeks later I was struck with a vision to have him on the front cover of this book. I shared some of the writing of this book with both Ken and Robert that night.

Some months later Brooks shared his vision with me that he knew before the season began that something special was in the offing in '95 for the Packers, the fans, the community, and himself. Wearing a Nike-swished black beret and a neat long-sleeved gray sweater, he made his way into the studio. I was taking a call on the phone when he caught my eye. The moment I met Robert, I could feel his love for people. I could tell within minutes of being near him that this was a very special young man. With due respect to all of the players, Brooks may be the most approachable player on the Green Bay Packers. I sensed this quickly as I began talking to him.

"Robert, what's it like jumping into the arms of those fans after a touchdown?" I asked.

"Man, it's great. There just isn't a better feeling than being up there with those fans going crazy."

"Are they saying anything to you?"

"You really can't hear anything. Everybody is just shaking you and stuff."

"Robert, you take off way out from the bleachers. Are you ever worried you're not going to make it?"

"When you got the adrenaline flowing, you know you're gonna make it," he said with a great big smile.

There was a high jumper one time who, when asked how he was able to make a world record jump, said, "It was easy. I just threw my heart over the bar, and the rest of my body followed." It's the same with Robert Brooks.

As the interview continued, love, care, and concern for his teammates and the fans oozed from the trim wide receiver. Robert explained that he had made some key decisions before the season in regards to his spiritual life, namely his relationship with God.

Far from spotless, Robert knows that as a Christian, he's not perfect —just forgiven. "I fall sometimes and I have flaws, but God forgives me. It's not a sin to fail, but it is to not get back up, but it takes faith." Brooks decided to get back up and follow the Lord.

"My relationship with the Lord has moved to another level this year. Last year, I was doing some stuff I shouldn't have been doing, and I was having bad luck. I had a pulled muscle and the heart thing. In my heart, I knew I was keeping me from being blessed."

In a matter of a decision things turned around.

"I rededicated my life to the Lord, and I started to pray to God, 'Give me a sign and let me know You're taking over.' It took a little while, but seven weeks later, my hamstring healed, and I ran a punt back for a touchdown, and I knew that was God talking to me. I hadn't told anyone, but I just knew. By drawing closer to the Lord, I feel He has blessed me."

That was an understatement.

Brooks told of another powerful spiritual experience during the 1995 season. "Before the '95 Falcon playoff game at Lambeau Field, Steve Newman (Packer chaplain) came up with a great verse of scripture from Hebrews 10 that really caught my heart, and I wrote it on my shoe."

I interrupted, "Robert do you mean to tell me that you were out there in that game *standing* on the word, and then, with a *leap of faith* you took it to the fans?"

Ken and Robert both burst into laughter.

Before "Reggie White Miracle Two", the hamstring reparation, Brooks was the greatest evidence that God's hand was on, in, and around the Green Bay Packers as he threw his big heart below his helmet into the crowd. This act, whose positive effect couldn't be seen on the scoreboard, brought something immeasurable to the Green Bay Packers, and the fans. And humbly Brooks says he can't take all the credit.

"There was an attitude and atmosphere that existed from top to bottom with the team. In 1995, nobody cared who got the ball or who was going to get the credit. Coach Holmgren just brought the family atmosphere to another level," said the speedy receiver. "Coach said, 'We're going to spend a lot of time together. We *can* win—and we *will* win, but we need to do it as a family—no matter what happens.' "

The Packers did win, and they successfully accomplished it as a family and for their family in the seats and those at home.

Thanks in huge part to Brooks, the Packer-fan bond and enthusiasm has reached epidemic proportions. The heartwarming sight of Brooks and other Packers leaping into the loving arms of the Cheeseheads after touchdowns has become a ritual. Faithful diehards in snowmobile suits and deer hunting outfits brave the cold, sitting in the front rows waiting to snag the "Lambeau Leaper." Looks of pure pride, anticipation, and exuberation radiated on their faces.

If Brooks and other Packers were fish, they might never have been thrown back. The fans love this new touchdown tradition, and so do the players!

Things in the Packer fan neighborhood have changed over the years. Instead of a man freezing Sunday afternoons ice fishing on Lake Winnebago, the guy now comes home from the Packer game and says, "Honey, guess what I caught today?"

"What?"

"Robert Brooks!"

"It just doesn't get any better than jumping into the arms of those fans. It's just a natural reaction now after a touchdown. I start dashing through the end zone to spend some time with the greatest fans in the world who pay our salaries and love us so much," said Brooks.

Peter King is certain of one thing. "If the Packers had beaten Dallas in the NFC Championship and the Packers would have won the Super Bowl, I believe, after Brett, the story would have been about Robert Brooks jumping into the stands. Robert Brooks seemed to be saying, 'Take me, I'm yours!'"

How did this jumping thing all start anyway? Robert remembers it very vividly. "Before the season, I told LeRoy Butler that I was going to jump into the stands, just like he did." Butler had first leapt into the arms of the Cheeseheads during a Lambeau Field contest with the Raiders in 1993. Reggie White had picked up a fumble and lateraled to Butler who took it the last distance for the touchdown and then set the precedent.

Unlike Brooks's '95 vaults, Butler kind of stuck to the wall like a magnet to a refrigerator door as the fans tugged on him. Little did he know at the time that he had started something that will go down in Packer history and the NFL's as well.

Brooks had just a few minor adjustments in mind for his leaps, and then he put them into action. "I said, 'I'm gonna jump all the way into the stands, not just hang on the wall.' " Robert kept his word, even though he knew there were some risks involved. "I knew there was the possibility of getting a penalty or fine from the league, and Coach Holmgren getting mad at me, but I wanted to do something to fire everybody up." It did, and somewhat surprisingly, he didn't get fined.

And even Coach Holmgren loved it! "As long as they throw him back, I think it's great," said the Packer head coach.

This new tradition had a tremendous effect on the team and the great Packer fans. To minimize this fact would be like saying the *Titanic* had a small leak. Precedent had been set, according to Packer President and CEO Bob Harlan. "No matter who does this in the future, everybody knows and will say, 'Hey, that started in Green Bay!' "

Even if the league decided to halt this new tradition of leaping into the stands, Robert's not sure he could resist. "Right now, it's just instinct. I'm sure a few times I'd go and do it without even thinking, but I just hope they don't every take this away. I love doing it."

Even more than being a good football player, Brooks is an even greater person. Brooks brings to the Green Bay Packers what very few can bring. There are a lot of talented athletes in the world, but Brooks is hard working, goal-oriented, and fully focused every down he plays. Speaking of downs, probably one of the greatest things about him is he is always down-to-earth. His meek spirit and humble attitude make him one of the most lovable, approachable players in the National Football League, and his popularity, like the Packers, is on the rise. When he's done playing football, I'm sure the Packers can still use him, not on the football field, but in public relations. He's doing both right now.

But those aren't his only skills. Brooks also serves as team barber, and he owns his own record company.

Sean Jones said, "I think we might have to boycott Robert a bit with the haircuts. His prices are getting a little high," he laughed.

Joe Kelly, who played for the 1995 Packers, was taking a stab at it too, and Brooks noticed.

"There are a few quacks out there, but I'm the main guy," he said.

So not only is Brooks Brett Favre's go-to guy on the field, but apparently he's the go-to guy in the hair chair as well.

Self-taught on keyboards, Brooks is releasing a song, "Jump." On the front cover of the CD is a picture of him jumping into the stands at Lambeau Field.

Speaking of getting and going up, Mike Gousha, from WTMJ-TV-4, in Milwaukee asked Brooks, "Do you ever have any fear jumping up into the stands?"

"No, not at all," Robert said without hesitation or reservation. "Especially in Green Bay. They're the greatest fans in the world."

All things considered, it really is an act of faith for Brooks every time he makes his Nike-spiked launch.

Speaking of faith, sit down, put your feet up, close your eyes, lean back, and imagine this: The Packers are in the Super Bowl, and it's overtime. Brett Favre spots Brooks over the middle in the end zone. Zing! Touchdown! Without breaking stride, Brooks heads for the back of the end zone. He launches.

When it happens, it will be the leap seen round the world.

It's gonna happen. It's not a matter of if, but when. And if you think Green Bay is the closest thing to heaven now, Lord help us all on that day! Packer fans, along with Robert Brooks, take a leap of faith and believe it will happen, and it will, probably in 1996!

President of the Green Bay Packers, Inc., and Chief Executive Officer of the corporation, BOB HARLAN has guided the Packer organization since 1989, leading it back to respectability in the NFL.

☰hree

It Starts at the Top

A lot of things about the Green Bay Packers just don't make sense. I mean, how could a team go through a 20-year losing drought from the early '70s to the early '90s and still nearly pack the stadium every game? And nearly as puzzling as why we park on driveways and drive on parkways is how the Packer season ticket list has increased by the thousands during this time. There's only one simple answer: an undying loyalty by the greatest fans in the world—Packer fans.

It started at the top with the original Packer forefathers, and today Bob Harlan, president and CEO of the corporation that operates the Packers, has his finger on the pulse of the Pack, making sure that the team continues to do everything that's right in a league where a lot has gone wrong. You can even catch this from Hawaii.

Ford Lewis of the *Honolulu Advertiser* sees it like this: "Simply, the Packers are everything the Dallas Cowboys aren't, and the Indianapolis Colts can never be. They are a team of history." Lewis goes a step further: "In Green Bay when the players go into the stands, it's in celebration, not anger. The Cowboys might be 'Corporate America', but the Packers remain what they've always been: the people's team."

From the early years of their existence, the Green Bay Packers have been structured to be very unique. The organization that operates the Packers is a privately held, not-for-profit corporation of stockholders who are the descendants of the community-minded businesspeople who saved the Packers from extinction on more than one occasion. In a sense, the people of Green Bay and environs own the Packers, and this makes this lovable small-town America team one of a kind in the 30-club NFL.

We hate to pick on the Cowboys—okay, we kind of enjoy it—but this next observation didn't come from Green Bay. Larry Guest of the *Orlando Sentinel* wrote: "The Cowboys play in an urban sprawl knitting so many municipalities. They call it the Metroplex. The Packers play in a town. The Cowboys are owned by the pushiest, dollar grubbingist, me-first egomaniac this side of George Steinbrenner. The Packers are owned by their fans, 1,898 stockholders, to be precise."

Founded in 1923, the corporation consists of 4,634 shares of stock owned by 1,898 stockholders. Shareholders are spread out over all 50 states and three foreign countries.

Lee Remmel, Packer director of public relations, believes that this is very significant. Remmel said, "Being publicly owned, many of the fans claim the 'we' tag, not 'they,' here in Green Bay. Even though they do not have a financial interest in the team, they feel like they do. This is a good thing. We believe this is one of the things that make Packer fans feel like a part of the team."

It is an undeniable fact that this organization cares about their players, employees, community, and their fans.

For the players, the Packers have recently created the post of director of family relations. Bob Harlan said, "We have a (person) on staff who helps the players from the time they get to Green Bay until they leave. If they need assistance in finding and purchasing a home, need a dentist, or anything, we're there to help. Maybe they need help moving, whatever, we want to help."

It's no wonder that the people in this organization, from the players on the field to the man who cleans the carpet, don't seem to ever leave the Green Bay area. Harlan said, "People don't leave here. They usually wind up staying here until they retire."

Just how far does the team go to make everyone on the staff a part of the family? During the 1995 playoffs, the organization flew the entire office staff to Dallas for the NFC Championship.

Former Packer Larry McCarren found this pretty impressive. "In a world where corporate America says, 'You're a part of the team,' but doesn't back it up, this team 'walks the talk' by showing it."

The Packers annually throw a Christmas party for everyone. Does it really matter if the Green Bay Packer organization throws this party for everyone from the parking lot attendant to the front office? Does it make a difference that Edie Wolf, wife of GM Ron Wolf, sends birthday cards to all the members of the Packer family at her own expense?

It's no secret that this organization treats their people like they want to be treated. It's no secret that probably more than 50% of all employees in this country, and around the world, would just as soon have their boss stand up in front of their co-workers and praise them than have a $500 bonus.

Jim Van Matre from the Green Bay Conventions and Visitors Bureau talked of how the community-related focus by the Green Bay Packers organization makes a huge investment in the local and state spirit as well as the economy. Van Matre explained: "The Packers care about the local community and have taken great effort to help the local service clubs. *Every* concession stand in Lambeau Field is staffed by volunteers who proudly provide the labor force."

This 45-year tradition that has included nearly 70 service clubs, from the Kaukauna Athletic Club to the Luxemburg Casco Jaycees, helps raise money, and the team benefits as well.

"It's a real plus for several different reasons. For management, they know that the labor needs of the concessions are taken care of, and for the service clubs, it's great too," said Van Matre.

The Packers love and care about their fans. If there was ever an organization who could take advantage of and gouge their fans, it could be the Green Bay Packer club, but they'll have no part in that.

As of 1996, even with a slight ticket increase to give more revenue to the visiting teams, the average ticket price for a game at Lambeau Field is just $28.17—next to last in the NFL! When the organization talks about providing entertainment for a good price, they mean it.

It should be noted that the Green Bay Packers have sold out regular season games for years and years. The Packer season ticket waiting list mentioned earlier has a list of names that stretches from here to the moon. Specifically, it is near 23,000 and growing!

The Green Bay Packers have always been very fiscally responsible, despite the fact there isn't an owners check book to load up. The Packers had a net income of nearly $4.5 million in 1995, nearly a million dollars more than their best year of $3.3 million in 1994.

So just who is the head of this admirable, impressive organization and Packer family? With whom does the buck start? Where does it stop? It starts with Bob Harlan, who deserves a lot of the credit but don't expect him to take it. Let's take you through the family chain.

BOB HARLAN, President and CEO

The pace of the pack (pun intended) is the pace of the leader. And with the Green Bay Packers, it starts at the top with Bob Harlan, the president and CEO of the franchise. He has been involved in the organization's front office since 1971. His duties are to oversee the whole Packer administration. He was elected to his post by the shareholders and directors.

The family feeling that exists between the fans and players comes as no surprise. With a background in public relations, Harlan is a firm believer in the importance of ongoing, person-to-person dialogue with the team's fans. In a world where it's tough getting appreciation from the local business down the street, Bob Harlan instituted "Breakfast with the Packers". Fans are selected at random by computer, and Harlan invites questions and feedback from them about the Packer organization.

With a full stadium and a nice balance in the checkbook, why does this organization care so much about their fans?

Harlan responded: "These fans have been so loyal throughout the years, and this team and organization loves and appreciates them very much. They are a part of us."

Harlan makes no secret that he has one of the greatest jobs in the world. "It's a privilege because of the history and the tradition. What's happened in Green Bay *can't* and *won't* ever happen again because of the size of the town and the structure. We're what America used to be and simply isn't anymore."

Bob Harlan proudly acknowledges that during an NFL meeting during the off-season, one of the owners said something that made him feel good. He said, "The Packers are the purest team in the league, you're owned by the fans, you can't move, and there's no owners pockets to stuff."

Indeed, it starts at the top with Harlan. What other president of a professional football team returns all his calls personally? Matter-of-fact, he answers his own telephone!

RON WOLF, Executive Vice-President and General Manager

On November 27, 1991, Bob Harlan made one of the most ingenious moves in Packer history. He moved the executive committee to hire Ron Wolf as executive vice-president and general manager.

Hats off to Wolf and the whole Packer organization for putting an emphasis on not just drafting and hiring good football players, but good people too. There's no doubt that this has played into the recent success of the team.

According to Wolf, the great chemistry on the 1995 team was a result of what he called "the great character of the individuals on the team." It's been said that "the whole is greater than the sum of it's parts." One great player does not a make a good football team. But Ron knows that where there is character, there is discipline, and where there is discipline, there are champions.

In Wolf's words, "Each potential draftee player is evaluated with careful scrutiny in disclosing the type of person each individual player is. We don't want losers here."

MIKE HOLMGREN, Head Coach

A man of strong faith and commitment to family values, Mike Holmgren, hired in 1992 by Ron Wolf, arrived in Green Bay to take on one of the toughest, yet most enjoyable head coaching jobs in the world. To say that Packer fans are not constantly positively expectant is like saying the Hindenberg suffered a slight mechanical failure upon landing. With this in mind, Holmgren took the job anyway.

The coach is a hit with the fans, and his players enjoy him too. Ken Ruettgers, for one, will tell you that he was on his way out of town after the 1991 season. Holmgren rejuvenated his career through words of support.

Keith Jackson said, "Coach Holmgren is the type of guy who won't point fingers directly at players and embarrass them. He gets his point across. You know if he's referring to you. But he does it so well and constructively."

Holmgren isn't one to beat around the bush. Former Packer Charles Jordan appreciated this great trait of the coach. "You now where you stand with him," said Jordan during the 1995 season, his last as a Packer.

Holmgren takes winning off-the-field as important as on. Early in the 1995 season, Ken and Sheryl Ruettgers appeared on Holmgren's television show to talk about something more important than football: life after it. Taking time away from discussing the normal game happenings and the like, they discussed a special program called "Invest In Yourself". Totally unique to the NFL, this program reaches out to help Packer players who choose to participate learn about handling life during and after their careers, long or short.

It's been noted that up to 75% of professional football players, as recent as two years out of the game, are either divorced, unemployed, or bankrupt, and Mike Holmgren and the Packers don't like those odds. Packer management is doing their part to fight the odds, and prove that every Packer is more than just a football player.

THE ORGANIZATION

We know that it's important to have a team and organization of integrity, but just how important is it to provide a winner in this or any other professional sport? Does it really have an effect on the community one way or another? The answer to this question is yes, and here's why.

When you have a popular, winning organization that sells hot dogs, this employs people. It doesn't hurt the local economy when motels are full either. They all play a big part in continuing to build pride and loyalty. That's what exists in Green Bay.

If there were a trial held to build a case that the Green Bay Packer football club does things in an integral, family way, they'd have to be unanimously pronounced "guilty" as charged. They continue to go the extra 100 yards in their commitment to the players, off-the-field, as well as on, their employees, community, and fans.

Unfortunately, this attitude hasn't arrived in Green Bay, or anywhere else where it exists, without cost and pain. Many of the lessons we all learn from come from adverse results and that won't be denied.

Football, like any other professional sport, hasn't been without casualties.

Have the owners, management, players, and coaches learned their lessons and employed these principles, laws, and philosophies to their teams by default? Have they come to realize that God's way—and the

Packer way truly is God's way—is the only way to govern and teach?

Teams and their players have found things seem to go better on the field when there is love in the home. That goes for winners of the Super Bowl, World Series, NHL championship, and NBA title as well.

It's difficult to imagine Mike Holmgren enforcing with fervor Vince Lombardi's famous quote: "Winning is not everything, it's the only thing." In fairness to the late coach, he might have been overemphasizing the point for dramatic reasons.

How important is winning? Are the Packers tired of going to Dallas every year and getting their helmets and the fans hearts crushed? Any fan will admit that the Cowboys are a bit of a sore subject at present. The Packers have been unfortunate enough to play the star-helmeted 1995 Super Bowl champs about 15 times in the last two seasons. (Actually only six meetings from 1993 to 1995. It just seems like more.)

Who are the these Cowboys? Well, the Cowboys play at a stadium in Texas with half a roof and a hard surface covered with astroturf. Troy Aikman is their quarterback; Deion Sanders is their main spokesman; and their flamboyant owner is Jerry Jones.

Many find it hard to believe that our country as a whole is really thrilled with the Jerry Jones's Cowboy mind set, even though it leads to championships. Arguably, the Cowboys may be America's team, but the Packers look like God's team!

I think there may be a thread of evidence that things are done a little bit differently in Dallas than in Green Bay, but I don't know for sure.

The Dallas Morning News reported that Jerry Jones, a multi-million-aire, wears conservative suits, stays in $1,500-a-day hotel suites, and has a couple limousines at his beck and call, a private jet, the whole shebang.

There was one observation made during the article in the paper that I thought was very significant. It said that although Jones could afford to lavish himself with diamonds and gold, he doesn't. He does, however, sport only one piece of jewelry: a Super Bowl ring. They add that the round, gold Super Bowl ring on his left hand is *so* big, there isn't even room for his wedding band! What a shame.

Now, I don't know if you heard the same message I did with that comment, but let me translate.

Jerry Jones is married. Jerry Jones also is the owner of a football team, a very good team, one of the best teams on the face of the earth right now. But he does have this one problem: His Super Bowl ring is *so* big that he can't even find room on his hand to wear his wedding ring and acknowledge the fact that he's married. Really loves his wife, doesn't he?

Does that make a statement about Jones's values and priorities?

If I happen to be inaccurate in my assumption of Jones's priorities, then I stand corrected and will personally allow the Cowboy honcho to pick me up in his private jet, put me up in one of those fancy suites, carry me around in his limo, give me tickets to a couple Dallas games, and then I will humbly apologize to him personally. I can admit I'm wrong to anyone—except my wife.

Seriously, does this mean Jerry Jones is a bad person? No, I didn't say that. Do I believe he may have a different list of personal priorities than many in the Green Bay Packers organization? Yes. Does he have a better football team than the Packers, right now? Maybe.

Jesus Christ said, "Where your treasure is, there is your heart."

If you spend enough time with a person or organization, you can find their treasure or what is important to them. We are talking of that something that clearly reveals a person's or company's purpose—revealed by the fruit of their philosophy.

Here's a little story about the heart and treasure of the Green Bay Packer organization, shared by Peter King in an article in *Sports Illustrated.*

Welcome to the Green Bay Packer Conference Room on the second floor of the Packer offices held a special gathering. It's Friday afternoon, October 20, 1995. Mail clerk Leo Yelle was having a birthday. The Packer organization helped him celebrate it. Nearly 40 secretaries and other office people were there eating cake and sipping refreshments. Included in the crowd were Bob Harlan, Brett Favre, and Peter King.

Leo Yelle is a very special person. He was receiving a special celebration. Some of the secretaries were off in the corner shedding tears, watching Leo admire the attention.

As the group began to depart, Peter King on his way out walked next to Bob Harlan and commented, "You know, this isn't like any other franchise."

Harlan just smiled.

We agree with you Peter. God help us if we ever forget it.

Something scary has erupted in the NFL as of late. It's caused a lot of concern around the league—including Green Bay. Teams have begun to move to other cities. Even the Cleveland Browns, who had a great fan base who went to the "Dog Pound" to cheer them on, have not only moved to Baltimore, but they've changed their nickname to the Ravens. If it can happen to Cleveland, can it happen to Green Bay? It could, but it won't. Why? We went to Bob Harlan for the answer and hopefully some reassurance this won't ever happen with the beloved Pack.

Harlan said, "One of the best things that ever happened to the Green Bay Packers as far as keeping the franchise in existence were in the early 1960s when former commissioner Pete Rozelle was able to convince the owners to share the national television revenue. Last year, TV revenue was 60% of our total revenue. It's our lifeblood."

Next time we're complaining while sitting through that slew of network commercials, maybe we should keep this in mind.

The board of directors and Bob Harlan, and his family in the front offices on Lombardi Avenue in Green Bay care about the fans. In Title-town, the family tree is large. It's roots are deep; very deep. From Bob Harlan to "Joe Fan," the family tree is broad, it's branches blanket Wisconsin, the United States of America, and even into other countries. It starts at the top. Like none other, this family tree grows and spreads from high above, where God reigns, and He rains on it a lot of love—allowing it to bear much fruit, sweet tasty fruit which millions of lucky Green Bay Packer fans get to enjoy.

Quarterback BRETT FAVRE and head coach MIKE HOLMGREN confer on the sidelines.
Photo by Jim Biever.

$\mathbb{F}$our

Packermania:
An Epidemic With No Cure!

 man looks very uneasy in his easy chair. It's about 11:00 a.m. on an October Sunday. His face lacks color. He's crabby. He refuses to eat lunch. He looks drained.

His wife watches him from nearby. She wonders to herself, Maybe it's a nip of the flu that's been making it's way indiscriminately throughout the area. Was it the "7-Layer Packer Stew" he had last night? Are his green and gold underwear in a bunch? What's wrong with him? Any other Sunday, at this time, he's like a kid in a candy store.

She musters the courage and tippy-toes lovingly over to his chair. Gazing into her man's eyes, she inquires, "Honey, what is it? You're just not yourself today. I hate to see you this way."

He gathers his strength, turns to her with the look of a boy who has lost his puppy dog, and remarks, "It's BYE week!"

Yes, it's that tragic week during the season when a Packer fan, by no choice of his own, must go without Packer football for a week. It's a devastating challenge. Two-hour root canals are more enjoyable. We're talking serious discomfort for Packer die-hards.

"Thank goodness this only happens once a season!" he moans to his wife. "I can't take it!"

Known around Packerland and the medical community as P.W. (*Packers Withdrawal*), it's very prominent during this awful day each year. This yearly epidemic brings a sickening group of symptoms, witnessed in the hapless Packer fan. Luckily, this form of Packer virus is curable. Remarkably, the sufferer somehow rebounds drastically by kick-off of the Packer game the following week. Even though *Packers With-drawal* is temporary, you wouldn't wish it on your worst enemy.

Maybe you have just seen yourself in the person above. You're not alone. This Packer allegiance and loyalty thing is serious. It grasps the inner part of your being and won't let go. I've suffered through it for nearly 30 years. It all started with names like Starr, Hornung, and Nitschke.

After the '60s bunch, we came to adore John Brockington and Johnny Gray in the 1970s. Then we learned to love Lynn Dickey and Paul Coffman in the '80s. Today, on the big screen, we have reached new heights with Reggie White, Brett Favre, and Ken Ruettgers. Packermania is on the rampage!

In Wisconsin, you can find Packer die-hards at many sports establishments, including the 50 Yard Line in Green Bay, Moose O'Malley's in Appleton, Jerry's Place in Oshkosh, or Major Goolsby's in Milwaukee.

At times Packer fans feel like the people in the Kellogg's Frosted Flakes commercial. They don't want to acknowledge or admit how deeply they're hooked, but it happens with regularity here in Wisconsin.

Beth Ziarnik from Oshkosh says, "The Packers become a part of your being; they weave into the fabric of your life. In Wisconsin, they are a part of our culture and heritage. Without the Packers, we'd be lost."

Packer products sell everywhere. It certainly isn't because of the size of Green Bay or the local area where the heart of the fans reside. In reality, there are more people in many suburbs of Los Angeles and New York than in the whole city of Green Bay, which has nearly 100,000 residents.

So what is it that draws Packer fans from all over the world? There are plenty of opinions from many who have followed the team up close for some time.

Bob McGinn, head sportswriter for the *Milwaukee Journal Sentinel,* has some ideas. "You have the rural small-town thing. The nation has sort of taken the team under it's wing. It's like David and Goliath. Green Bay is David, and the big cities are the Goliath's. A lot of people are looking to root for the underdog." He continues, "In Wisconsin, nothing compares with the Packers. There is no denying this team has an irresistible, romantic allure about it."

A little bit of fudge is good; too much can give a stomach ache; and even too much sunshine burns. But Packer fans can't get enough of their team. Are Packer fans a little off their rockers? Are they there for better or worse, for rich or poor, in sickness and in health? You better believe it! The love affair is a marriage made in heaven with the chance of divorce between fan and team nearly zilch! The same can't be said about the marriage of some of the fans. Packermania has literally caused temporary blindness in some homes.

Peggy, a Packer Widow, tells this true story. "I got so tired of Howie's lack of attention for me during Packer games that I came up with an idea that I was sure would reach him. During the second quarter of a Packer game, I fixed my hair, put on my finest evening gown, and a half a bottle of perfume—the works. During the halftime entertainment and the highlights, I very subtly walked in front of the TV. He didn't even notice me. Even if he couldn't see me, the perfume should have knocked him off his chair. It didn't. I was worried. I thought maybe he was dead. Not one to give up easily, I stood blocking the TV screen, looked into his eyes with the spirit of Mae West and said, 'Why don't you come up and see me sometime?'

"There was no reaction; virtually no sign of life. He sat with a blank stare.

"In a last ditch effort I went over and sat on his lap leaned with my cheek to his nose and asked, 'Do you know what kind of perfume this is?'

" 'Midnight At The Landfill' ... I don't know,' he replied stuffing a hot dog in his face. 'Excuse me, dear, I gotta go out to the kitchen and get something to drink. The second half's about to start.' "

I'm sure Peggy's story is not an exclusive. Trying to penetrate the "Twilight Zone" of a Packer nut's mind can be futile. On a positive note, Peggy learned over the years, reconciliation was usually sped up by a Packer victory.

Vern Biever has spent over 40 years right smack dab in the middle of the Green Bay Packers. He is the official sideline photographer for the team. Vern and his son Jim are two of only six people who have been on the sideline shooting pictures for every Super Bowl ever played. He's been in every NFL stadium and has some real good ideas why Packermania isn't limited to just Wisconsin.

"A kid in Mississippi, for example, takes a look at all of the NFL teams and says, 'Hey, let's follow this team in Green Bay.' There is more of a tendency to pull for the small town than big cities like New York or Los Angeles."

According to Biever, there are no fans like Packer fans. "They are the greatest—they are fanatics. You simply can't imagine how many Packer fans there are in other towns. It would astound you."

Bill Jartz, a Green Bay TV sports personality, agrees with Vern. He has a colorful picture of the people he has found himself in the center of for many years. "Packer fans are knowledgeable, rabid, but classy. I am always amazed by the huge number of fans at the hotels and airports. Without a doubt the Packers are truly 'America's Team.' "

Bill has confidence in the Packers, and their Packermania-laced fans. "The next step will be the big one. When we win the Super Bowl, there will be no Detroit riots in Green Bay," he points out.

It is a fact that the Packers' hat size has remained relatively the same over the years, but until the last few years, there weren't a lot of wins to have their heads swell so much that it would affect the size of the cheesehead hats that blanket Packerland.

Larry McCarren, another TV Sports Personality in Green Bay and a former Packer, remembers many of those lean years and the loyalty of the fans through them. McCarren, a native of Illinois, was proud to wear Packer green and gold from 1973 to 1984. He made the world's fastest transition from a Bear fan to a Packer fan when the Packers drafted him back in 1973. "Right after I hung up the phone with the Packers, it was a 180-degree turn," he recalled.

Today, McCarren, in front of the camera, a far cry from his days in the trenches anchoring the offensive line, shared some memories. "Even when we (the Packers) were lousy, the fans came out to watch us. Not only at home, but everywhere we went to play, there was always a pocket of Packer fans yelling and screaming for us." He makes one other intriguing statement about the team. "The Packers are the Notre Dame of the National Football League." (John Winn of Oshkosh made me put that in, but McCarren did say it.)

Even up until the last few years, when Packer wins became more frequent, you never heard of anyone burning their Packer shirts, banners, or other allegiance supporting apparel. And when they were losing, you didn't see Packer fans wearing paper bags over their heads at games. It just don't and won't happen with Packer fans.

Today, we homespun Packers fanatics blessed with the Packermania virus are known as "Cheeseheads" to much of the nation. There was a guy who was spared serious injury by using his foam cheesehead hat to cushion a blow during a plane crash. He was on national television, and even the Cowboys made sure he had tickets to the 1996 Super Bowl. The Cowboys!

The media, mainly the game day TV cameras, seem bent on trying to convince most people around the world that all of us Packer fans sit in the stands with our faces painted green and gold with no shirts on in the middle of winter with a beverage in hand. Some of us are wise enough to dress warm and are a little more even keeled, but we admittedly have our moments also.

For Packer fans, the aroma of bratwurst, burgers, eggs and bacon, or other culinary delights which fill the air of the parking lot at Lambeau Field hours before games is the scent of heaven. Tailgating before kickoff and after the final gun makes a Packer game an event, a happening.

But not all great Packer fans can be found in Lambeau Field. Not everyone chooses to face the pre-game traffic congestion or make the necessary tailgate preparations for seeing a game in person. Some feel the prices are a little better at home, the line is shorter to the bathroom, and it's usually warmer there in December.

To think there was a time when Packer tickets were easy to come upon is almost inconceivable today. Packermania entered it's early stages when Lombardi, Starr, Hornung, and Nitschke arrived in Green Bay. Although the seats at Lambeau were full, it was still a challenge to watch the Packers play in many homes near by. The NFL sometimes blacked out the games from TV viewers in the Green Bay area in the early 1960s, despite a sold out Lambeau Field. It wasn't unusual for fans to drive to as far away as Sheboygan to watch the games. The blackout covered nearly a 100-mile radius. Packer fans would not then—and still today—refuse to be denied from watching their team. Satellite dishes have come to the rescue for many Packer fans.

The Packer bug bites hard and deep, and it's wonderful effect is a friendly virus which results in Packermania. With some, not only is it unshakable, but nearly deadly.

Greta Van Susteren, originally from Appleton, Wisconsin, flew onto the national scene recently with CNN. (She did commentary for the O.J. Simpson trial.) Although she works in Washington, D.C., she's still loaded with a healthy dose of Packermania. "Being a Packer fan is like a disease, it's terminal, it never leaves you!"

Back in the '60s, Van Susteren remembers literally being lifted up by a few of the Packer teddy bears. "At Fuzzy Thurston's Left Guard Restaurant, Herb Adderly and Lionel Aldridge would put me on their shoulders and carried me around. They were so big and so nice."

Greta has taken her share of pokes from envious fans over the years. Matter of fact, she's married to a Colts fan. His name is John Coale. "He'd never admit it, but he really is a Packer fan. He still won't admit that Bart Starr was a better quarterback than Johnny Unitas," she says with a laugh.

At home in Green Bay, people are not just fans, but team members, the 12th man. Randy Cross, NBC-TV Football analyst, in a recent visit to a local sports banquet, said to about 4,000 fans, "Do you guys really love your team as much as it looks like you do on TV?"

There was an instant roar of affirmation.

He continued, "I played a few games in Green Bay. In December, your stands look like the world's largest duck blind!"

He was referring to all the fluorescent, hunting clothes worn in the November and December cold by fans in Lambeau Field or Milwaukee County Stadium.

Cross said he didn't know of any fans more deserving of a Super Bowl win than the Packers fans, or any other in their class, as well.

We agree.

The football player turned broadcaster concluded, "For every snowball throwing moron in New York, there are twenty great fans in Green Bay."

It's true.

What is it about this team that makes them such a great match for their loyal, loving fans?

The players in Green Bay haven't come to the place where they take their fans for granted, where they don't care about them. It's obvious that the friendship between player and fan is mutual. The fan cheers till his eyes fall out, while the players show exuberance by jumping into the crowd after touchdowns.

The Packer organization has done the best it can at keeping ticket prices reasonable. Their cost to do business increases just like any other, but they are to be commended. Even their latest price increase leaves them at second lowest in the league in average price per ticket.

Lord help us if the day comes where we lose the "us" attitude from the team, and it is replaced with "we" and "they". Heaven forbid if a fan would even considers throwing a snowball at a precious Packer member like Giants fans have done.

God forgive us all if we take each other for granted. This process has changed the lives of millions in a good way.

Just ask my wife Kim. Her lukewarm attitude about the Packers has changed since she was introduced to them nearly 13 years ago. Once a Packer pacifist, she's got plastic team decals with logos and stuff on mirrors, lamps, and on other furniture, normally not to be touched by human hands. Her Brett Favre autographed helmet takes up the top of the stereo.

On game day of the '95 opener against the St. Louis Rams, she grabs her Packer T-shirt out of her dresser drawer. She pulls on her green socks. Her black belt in shopping will hang in the closet. With her feet propped up in her recliner, with a bowl of popcorn on her lap, she tells me, "If you have anything to say, say it now. The Packer season is about to begin, otherwise it will have to wait till after the Super Bowl." Women and their football. When will they learn to understand that we men need their attention more than anything?

I ask myself, "Is this the same woman who was named to the First Team of the Sunday afternoon "All-Mall" team? The same green-eyed beauty who just years before was elected into the "Mastercard Hall of Fame"?

Through their magical powers, that bunch in Green Bay created a Packer monster that threatens to make a Packer widower of me!

"Pass me the milk, cheese, and butter," she exclaims.

Her beautiful hair that normally must not be mussed up in the least is slam-dunked by her cheesehead hat. She's planted herself firmly five feet in front of the TV. The answering machine is on; no phone calls will be taken. The laundry will wait. She's not going anywhere.

"This is going to be our year. The Niners and Cowboys are going down!" she proclaims, with a pumping fist from her arm chair in the living room.

A win on this day will bring jubilation and elation. A loss could take days for her to recover. Women and their football.

Is she insane? Possibly.

Are we all CRAZY ... about our Packers? Absolutely!

Kim and countless millions like her, through a leap of faith, are bound annually onto the Packer stage with the players. It's become an on-going, romantic love story, playing year around under God's direction. One that calls, "Action!" regularly convening at the corner of Lombardi and Oneida streets, in a little town called Green Bay.

Five

Cheeseheads:
The Greatest Fans
in the World

There has always been a mysteriously seductive, romantic attraction to the Packers that's beyond explanation. It has even drawn a few fans from the enemy camp. Growing up in Minnesota as a Viking fan, Jim Coursolle never dreamed he'd cross over.

In 1976, Coursolle, then 33, and his wife Diane moved to Wisconsin after purchasing a radio station in Waupun. It didn't take long for him to become a Packer fanatic. After a trip to the Hall of Fame in the late '70s, it was all over. 20 years later, he sports a 50,000-watt FM radio station in Oshkosh, Wisconsin, that backs the Pack.

How did this happen?

Said Coursolle: "I was watching this great film at the Packer Hall of Fame about the deep, rich Packer tradition. I was listening to Ray Scott. (Scott was the TV voice of the Packers.) His resonant voice boasted of this little town, in the middle of nowhere, that was able to maintain this franchise. It reminded me of the story as a kid called *The Little Engine That Could*."

Coursolle took his Packer allegiance a mighty step further when he put his money where his mouth is. Today you can tune in "Packer Radio" WPKR in Oshkosh, Wisconsin. It is the only radio station of it's kind with this unique affiliation and loyalty to a sports franchise anywhere. Coursolle has become a collector of "things Packer" and has put much of his collection on display in the two halls of the station. His "mini-Packer Hall of Fame" includes a portion of a goal post from the 1967 Ice Bowl, the oldest NFL program known to exist, and one of Vince Lombardi's warmup jackets. Hanging on one wall is his "million-dollar" contract from the Packers. It was given to him by Tom Braatz, who served as executive vice-president of football operations for the team in the '80s. Coursolle's favorite piece of memorabilia? "I have an unused ticket to the Ice Bowl. Millions of people said they were there. Well, I know one who wasn't because I got his ticket!" he roars.

Lee Remmel, Packer director of public relations and historian, says the Packers are impressed and warmed by Coursolle's devotion to the team. Said Remmel: "Jim's fanaticism for the Green Bay Packers is great. His allegiance demonstrated through his radio station is admired and appreciated by the Packer organization."

Today, Coursolle serves as a member of the board of directors for the Green Bay Packer Hall of Fame.

If you are ever in or near Oshkosh, tune in to WPKR, 99.5 on FM radio. The phone number is (414) 236-4242. If you call ahead, you might be fortunate to catch Jim on a slow day and get a free tour of his two halls of Packer collectibles.

Cheri Auctung, 18, spends her time serving customers in their cars at Gilles Drive In in Fond du Lac, Wisconsin. She proudly wears her Packer jacket on cool days. "They are a team with a lot of heart and spirit. There seems to be a magic about them. They are rough and tough football buffs," says Cheri.

If you think that it's just the guys who take this team seriously, think again. "I almost cry if I have to work when there is a football game on. When I wait on cars, many of them fill me in on what's going on."

So what happens when this young "Packer Monster" is watching the game on TV? "I get very keyed up during games. I only want to be a-round people who are serious about watching the game. I get upset if I don't hear everything the announcers say. I get mad at the ones who don't give the Packers enough credit," she says.

On Cheri's 18th birthday, her friends and family surprised her with a cake decked out in green and gold with the names and numbers of a few of her favorite Packers on it. The dessert was placed on a Packer tablecloth and devoured with green and gold forks and spoons.

Cheri is impressed with the Packers as football players, but more so as people. She also believes there has been a touch of God on the team. "I think God touched Green Bay the day that Reggie (White) felt his hamstring was good enough to play. It was truly a miracle for a man who is almost a miracle worker himself. Overall, I am very impressed with the players' faith in God."

Bill Schultz is a proud "Cheesehead". He came to Wisconsin from New England in 1993. Schultz spent a few years as a New England Patriots fan—until his arrival here when he quickly contracted a severe case of packermania. He claims there are some differences between the fans here and those in New England. "Packer Backers are full-time fans. They recall seasons, memories, and I can't believe how much green and gold they where here. It amazes me."

He goes a step further. "Fans know, recognize, and follow their players here. I saw a huge line of people in a restaurant waiting to get Packer kicker Chris Jacke's autograph. In New England, if two people in the 70,000 stadium knew the kicker' name it would be remarkable!"

Schultz confirms that the packermania epidemic is apparent to others around the country. He learned this when he and his wife Wendy took their new Packer pride home. "When I go back to the east coast friends ask, 'Is it really as much fun to be at the games as it looks like on TV? Do they like it when the players jump into the stands?' I assure them it is. They're jealous, I know," he says with a laugh.

From his time in Boston Red Sox land, Bill draws an interesting stadium parallel. "Lambeau Field is the Fenway Park of football stadia. In Boston, you have the big green monster. In Lambeau Field, you are embraced by the great traditions and memories. You see the names of the old players all over the stadium. It's awesome!"

Speaking of baseball for a bit, Chicago Cub fans may be the only ones comparable even to be mentioned as a close second to Packer Backers. Cub fans may have to take more of a leap of faith than Packer fans. At least the Packers have been to the big dance (Super Bowl) in the last 30 years. It's been an eternity for the Cubs. Noah had just gotten of the boat from the cruise the last time the Cubs were in the World Series. (Editor's note: Actually, it was 1945 when the Cubs were last in a World

Series, and they did make the Playoffs twice in the '80s.)

Ray Scott served as a play-by-play TV announcer assigned to cover the Packers from 1956 to 1967. Scott's voice is almost as synonymous with the Packers as Vince Lombardi. He is as much an authority on fans throughout the country as anyone. Scott says, "I'm biased, but Packers fans are the greatest in the world. I've had the privilege to see many, and there is no doubt, they are the finest."

Today, Scott still does a Wisconsin Packer TV Program, "Countdown to Kickoff", taped weekly during the season. Back home in Minnesota, you may find him quietly watching the Packers at Gabe's By the Park, a Packer fan haven in St. Paul.

Countless opinions like Scott's confirm there may be something to Green Bay's small town team mystique that draws fans to the Packers.

After growing up in Iowa with no specific allegiance to an NFL team, Perry Kidder arrived in Green Bay in 1979. "It took me ten minutes to become a Packer fan. They dominate here," he proclaims.

Shortly after he got here he was hooked by an experience that has clutched many others as well. "We were able to get some tickets, and I'll tell you what, walking into Lambeau Field was breathtaking. It was gorgeous."

When did Kidder realize that these fans were a bit different than others?

"I got a real indication of the depth of Packer fans when the loyalty never dropped even while they were losing. Fans care enough to get upset when they lose, but winning isn't important. They just love this team. It's not a game, it's a lifestyle here," he claims.

Packer fans will admit that they've taken their share of ribbing from other fans all over the country and even within Wisconsin. When the opportunity rose for Rich and Dorothy Leider and Jim and Kris Meyer, from Campbellsport, Wisconsin, to have some fun with a Detroit Lion fan and friend, they capitalized.

John Venturini took the brunt of some harmless fun. After the Packers beat the Steelers on Christmas Eve in 1995 to win the NFC Central Division crown from the Lions, the Leiders and Meyers paid a little visit to the Venturini's, who were out of town. Rich Leider recalls, "We painted a big yellow 'G' in the snow on their lawn, and we put green and gold streamers in the bushes and trees."

Before they were through there were balloons hanging from the mailbox and a huge sign on the garage door which read: "We Are The Champions, My Friend," a takeoff on a song from the '70s. This display was right near the "Thigpen for President!" poster on the house. (Yancey Thigpen, a Pittsburgh receiver, had dropped a sure touchdown pass with just seconds left that would have beaten the Packers and preserved the title for the Lions.)

Pam Werth, from tiny Markesan, Wisconsin, is one of the true believers of her Packers and the good Lord. Here's what she had to say when Reggie rebounded from his hamstring injury, which resurrected the team as well. "You know, God really wants us to win. Reggie was able to get healed and get back in there—he's got good connections!"

Author STEVE ROSE (left), ROBERT BROOKS, and author's mother, JEAN ROSE.

VINCE LOMBARDI brought leadership and discipline to Green Bay when he became the Packers' head coach in 1959. He also brought a degree of spirituality with him, leading his players by example and giving the Lord His due at all times.

Six

In Mysterious Ways

The people of Green Bay had followed their town team for more than two decades before Curly Lambeau came of age, took control of the local outfit in 1919, and got them a corporate sponsor, his employer, the Indian Packing Corporation, which was only natural because most of the players on the team worked for the same company. Thus, the town team came to be known as the Packers.

These first Packers succeeded on the field but not so at the box office. Once Lambeau entered the team into the professional league in 1921 expenses went up dramatically because in order to compete in the pro circuit he had to hire better players from outside the area. The first of these was Howard "Cub" Buck, a giant of a man with a heart of gold and a smile that made the sun jealous. Buck came to Green Bay, looked around a lot, liked what he saw, and stayed for five seasons as a player and several more as a business leader, Boy Scouts of America official, team official, and all-around good guy.

After Buck, came Verne Lewellen, a running back from Nebraska, who became a lawyer and district attorney for Brown County once his playing days were over. Along with Lewellen was Lavvie Dilweg, the fabulous end who had gone to Marquette before joining the Packers as a pro. Dilweg was elected to Congress by the voters of northeast Wisconsin.

Other players came and stayed and contributed greatly to the community in those early days, but the seeds of charity and fellowship were already growing to fruition before they started making their contributions to Green Bay.

The 1922 season was a miserable failure for Curly Lambeau's fledgling football corporation that was operating the Packers. Bad weather kept attendance down and the money coffers nearly empty all year long. Lambeau and associates were on the verge of bankruptcy when divine intervention broke their fall.

How can I be so certain that it was divine intervention? Well, like the famous Paul Harvey says, "And now the rest of the story."

It was Thanksgiving Day, and the sky was dumping rain on Green Bay again as it had so many times already that autumn. George Whitney Calhoun, the team's publicity man and a part owner in Lambeau's enterprise, went to the office that morning, even though it was a holiday. Calhoun worked for the *Green Bay Press-Gazette*, and one of his titles was wire editor; in other words, he checked the teletype wires for late-breaking stories that might be so great that the paper would have to get out a special extra edition in order to keep the public informed of the latest news.

The Packers had a game scheduled that day. It wasn't the original game that they set up for Thanksgiving Day; it was a fill-in affair with the Duluth Kellys because the NFL team that the Packers were supposed to play had canceled on them earlier in the week. Playing the Kellys was strictly for the money and not for the league standings.

Lambeau and Joe Ordens and Nate Abrams, two partners in his pro football venture, sought out Calhoun, the fourth and oldest man in the ownership group, to discuss whether they should go ahead with the game or should they cancel it because of the weather. If they played, attendance was bound to be low and it wouldn't be enough to pay the visiting team their guaranteed fee for coming. And if they didn't play, they would be risking their membership in the pro league because—non-league contest or not—canceling games was good cause for forfeiture of a franchise, something that Lambeau didn't want to face again; he'd already been through it the season before when he used college players in a league game and the NFL magnates forced the Clair brothers to give up the Green Bay franchise. What to do?

For some unknown reason, Andrew B. Turnbull, the newspaper's business manager, had gone to the office that morning as well. He didn't have to be there; he was the boss; he could stay home and enjoy the holiday with his family. But he was there, and for some other unknown reason, he went by Calhoun's office—which was out of his way—when he headed for home. He overheard Calhoun, Lambeau, Ordens, and Abrams talking, so he poked his head into the room. He knew all four men, but he also knew that this was the *Green Bay Press-Gazette* and not the corner coffee shop. Lambeau, Ordens, and Abrams shouldn't have been there. For another unknown reason, Turnbull ignored the rules and simply asked them what they were talking about. Calhoun filled him in. Turnbull saw their problem, and he advised them to play the game and not worry about the money. He wasn't sure why he was saying that, but he said it. Not worry about the money? He was the business manager for the newspaper; it was his job to worry about money. And now he was advising others not to worry about the money. What had gotten into him?

Lambeau and company took Turnbull's advice and played the game. Although the newspaper reported that nearly 2,000 fans turned out in a drizzle to see the Packers beat the Duluth Kellys, 10-0, the paying attendance was closer to 100 loyal Packer Backers, antecedents of those hardy souls who would brave sub-freezing temperatures in later years to watch their Packers defeat an NFL foe at Lambeau Field. The gate receipts weren't enough to meet expenses, and the little corporation fell farther into debt. All seemed lost.

Then the town came to the rescue—at the prodding of Andy Turnbull and a few of his close friends. They knew that a pro football team was good for the community, good for business, good for everybody; especially when it was a winner the way the Packers had always been.

Turnbull and his friends rallied financial support for Lambeau by forming a non-profit corporation that would take over business operation of the Packers. They sold stock at $5 a share, and the people of Green Bay became the owners of their own pro football team.

The first order of business was to pay off the debts of Lambeau's corporation, then help Lambeau field a team for the coming year. They succeeded in both areas, and the Packers were given new life.

Now for the rest of the story.

On Monday morning before Thanksgiving Lambeau received a telegram from the owner of the Packers' opponent for the Thanksgiving Day game in Green Bay. The greedy fellow demanded a guarantee of $4,000 to bring his team all the way to Green Bay to play on turkey day. Lambeau and associates didn't have that kind of money, and they didn't think attendance for the game would be good enough to raise that amount. They were left with no other alternative except to cancel the game with the big city team.

Not wishing to lose a prime playing date and thus miss a chance to make up some of their financial losses, the owners lined up a game with the Duluth Kellys, guaranteeing them a mere $1,000, which just an average crowd would cover and then some.

That Thanksgiving morning when it was raining Lambeau and his partners knew that the fans wouldn't come out in such foul weather to watch the Packers play a team from Duluth. They knew that the original big city team that had been on the schedule would have drawn a better crowd—even in the rain; but it still wouldn't have been big enough for the partners to pay the visiting team's guarantee demand. If the original team's owner hadn't been so greedy, the game with his big city team would have been played without any question. No meeting would have been held by the owners at the *Press-Gazette*, and Andy Turnbull and his friends wouldn't have intervened on behalf of the Packers.

Who was this greedy owner who started this series of minor events which have played such an enormous role in the history of the Green Bay Packers? Why, it was George S. Halas of the Chicago Bears who proved that the Lord moves in mysterious ways.

As Mr. Harvey says, "Now you know the rest of the story."

As an addendum, one question remains: Why did Turnbull and his friends succeed?

Just speculating here, but could it have been because the corporation that Turnbull and attorney Gerald Clifford set up in 1923 was done for the good of the community and not for personal gain? Could it have been that Lambeau's corporation was set up to make a profit for him and his fellow owners and that is why it failed? Could it have been that the second corporation succeeded because its charter included a clause that stated if the team did make money that the profits had to be given to charity?

I have to believe that God's hand was stirring this mix somewhere. Turnbull in the office on a holiday. Turnbull going by Calhoun's office when it was out of his way. Raining in Green Bay on November 30 when in most years it would have been snowing, which never kept anybody from going to a football game. Turnbull finding a lawyer who was willing to work for nothing to save the local football team. Turnbull and the officers of the new corporation running the Packers for no salary or any other sort compensation. If this doesn't sound like God had a hand in things, then at the very least these were very Christian men who put the good of the community ahead of themselves.

It was this Christian attitude that continued to draw players to Green Bay because until 1935 the NFL had no college player draft. After that, the players who were most likely to sign with the Packers were men of the same ilk who had preceded them in Green Bay uniforms. Men like Charley Brock, Buford "Baby" Ray, Walt Schlinkman, Dick Wildung, and the great Don Hutson.

Hutson's coming to Green Bay as a player is another one of those stories where God just might have had a hand in things. I suggest you read about it, as I did, in that wonderful series by Larry Names, *The History of the Green Bay Packers: The Lambeau Years, Part Two* (Angel Press of WI, 1990).

Then there's the incredible story of how the people of Wisconsin pulled together once again in the early 1950s to keep the Packers alive and in Green Bay for good. Larry Names retells it in the fourth in his series on the history of the Packers. Also in that volume, he relates how the people of Green Bay gave their overwhelming support to the building of a new stadium for the Packers in the mid-1950s.

Larry Names subtitled the fourth volume in the series: *The Shameful Years*, and probably not without good reason. The Packers were mostly atrocious on the field, but their play wasn't what he was referring to. It was some of the doings in the front office and behind the scenes that he was writing about. Fortunately for all of us today, those who would exemplify the Christian ethic won out.

As Larry Names has pointed out to me, Packer history is littered with many stories that can only be explained as divinely inspired or as the intervention of a heavenly hand. The Packers are proof that the Lord does move in mysterious ways.

BART STARR and JOHN GILLESPIE epitomized the Christian ethic when they worked hand-in-hand to establish Rawhide Boys Ranch in northeastern Wisconsin.

$\mathbb{S}$even

Glory Day Heroes

$\mathbb{T}$he bodies of the Green Bay Packers have always held charitable hearts, and long before Reggie White, Ken Ruettgers, Robert Brooks, and Brett Favre, a host of men arrived on the scene to pave a trail of benevolence in, around, and through Green Bay.

Those who know the story of Vince Lombardi might say that he was the first to bring personal integrity to Green Bay, but the incredible player-fan bonding we know today truly began even before his arrival in 1959 in Green Bay.

The newer generations remember how Lombardi restored winning ways to the Packers when he came to Green Bay in 1959. He not only brought back winning football to Wisconsin, he also brought back the pride in this professional football team that had gone astray over the previous decade. The continuing result is the most powerful allegiance in all of professional sports between team and supporters, coupled with a player-fan bonding tighter than a rusted cover on a jar of jam. It's also as consistent and as dependable as the sun rising in the east and setting in the west.

As a child growing up near Eden, Wisconsin, like thousands of other little kids with big dreams, my friends and I wanted to play for the Packers some day. We emulated our heroes in the back yard and on the playground. We pulled our pants to our knees to reveal our green socks. We wore plastic Packer helmets. We stuffed old rags under our shirts for shoulder pads. Some of us wanted to be the hard-nosed Ray Nitschke. Others wanted to make believe they could fly like the "Roadrunner", Travis Williams.

Sundays became very ritualistic during the Packer season. We went to church, came home, ate, and then sat like bunch of zombies with our eyeballs plastered to the TV.

Ingrained in my mind, I remember watching the green-and-gold take on Roman Gabriel's Los Angeles Rams, Johnny Unitas's Baltimore Colts, and Fran Tarkenton's Vikings then Giants. He later returned to the Vikings. We always won. (Well, almost always.)

Millions of us will admit it seems like just yesterday when Bart Starr was at quarterback. Jim Taylor, Paul Hornung, and Donny Anderson carried the ball. Jerry Kramer, Fuzzy Thurston, and Forrest Gregg anchored the offensive line. Carroll Dale and Boyd Dowler were the primary receiving targets. On defense, Willie Davis, the late Henry Jordan, Lionel Aldridge, and Ron Kostelnik formed the front wall. Ray Nitschke, with respect to Dick Butkus, was the fiercest linebacker in the league. Willie Wood and Herb Adderly picked off many passes in the defensive backfield. Don Chandler was the kicker.

We could identify our heroes by number in the twinkling of an eye. They appeared in color even though we watched them in black and white.

Without a doubt, Lombardi deserves his share of the credit for starting Packermania. No one will deny that building a winning team helped. But beyond just winning football games in Green Bay, Vince Lombardi was a great role model for many of his players.

Bob Skoronski, a '60s offensive linemen, recalls some things about his former coach. "Vince Lombardi really had a heart for people. His passion to win sometimes got lost in this, but he really cared about the people in Green Bay."

Bob continues his tribute to his former coach: "Back in the '60s when we played on Thanksgiving a lot, Vince always put on a great Thanksgiving dinner for the players and their families at the Green Bay American Legion Hall. Vince was an incredible host! He'd have movies for the kids and go around hugging them. He was a charmer with a real soft heart."

This image of Lombardi is far from the one many were shown in the newspapers and on television.

"Coach Lombardi even bought mink stoles, jewelry, and color television sets for player wives as a token of his appreciation for them. He knew that winning began in the church and home before it could be realized on the field. Vince was a great football mind, but he also emphasized the importance of getting to church and laying down good values and standards. Lombardi, who was a Roman Catholic, had great respect for everyone's faith."

Lombardi loved spending time with his family at home and members of his family of Packers, too. His relationship with his players varied. A lot depended on whether it was during the season or not.

Lee Remmel tells a family story that includes Lombardi, his men on the team, and even a hint that the "rugged one" may have even had a sense of humor:

"Vince did some deer hunting with the guys. One year some of his deer hunting buddies on the team bought him a florescent orange hunting jacket. He was visibly moved by the gift. He put it on. Then he got the message. As he took the jacket off, he noticed a huge bull's-eye the players had put on the back. He lost it ... fell on the floor laughing ... thought it was the funniest thing in the world."

This story relates a different man we got to know through the media. We thought he was all business. Is he really the one who supposedly said: "Winning isn't everything; it's the only thing."?

And so the '60s ushered great football into Green Bay and stories of Packer player generosity and benevolence as well.

Don Koepke and his wife Marion, from Appleton, served as volunteers on many local non-profit boards and committees with many of the early Packers. "Every time we made a plea to have a Packer help out, they showed up. A lot of the events were on the player's day off. They would be helping and pushing kids in wheelchairs," Koepke recalled, overcome with emotion. "It didn't matter whether they played regularly for the Packers or not, each one of them was first string when it came to community service."

Many NFL fans remember Bart Starr, the great Packer quarterback. More than a great football player, he was a wonderful family man in his home and the community. Take for instance the Rawhide Boys Ranch.

John Gillespie, founder and director of Development for the Rawhide Boys Ranch in New London, Wisconsin, remembers this touching story.

"God had laid on my wife Jan's and my heart to start a Ranch for delinquent boys. We heard that Bart and Cherry Starr had the same vision.

Jan said to me, `Why don't you call Bart?'"

Gillespie laughed to himself. His wife didn't seem to understand. This was August of 1965. The Packers were champions. Bart was very popular. "Honey, getting in touch with the Pope would be easier, plus he'll have an unlisted number."

"How do you know?" Jan echoed confidently.

"Trust me, I know."

Two weeks went by as John tried to get in touch with Starr through the back door. In the meantime, a piece of property came up for sale that John felt would be ideal for the ranch. There were offers on it, but the owner really wanted to see it become a Boys Ranch.

With his own leap of faith, Gillespie put a few thousand dollars down on the property. Keep in mind this was 1965. If you made $150 a week, that was big bucks. We're talking a lot of money, and the young Gillespies were carrying a big college debt.

Mrs. Gillespie persistently provoked her husband to try to call Starr. "Okay, I'll show you."

Gillespie called information and amazingly got Bart Starr's phone number.

"Jan, even if we do get a hold of him, he'll probably be too busy to meet with us," said her husband.

She persisted and he finally called Starr.

John recalls a man answering who simply said, "Hello."

"Is this the Starr residence?"

The voice said, "Yes it is."

"Is Mr. Starr home?

"There is no Mr. Starr here, but Bart is."

"That's who I want to talk to."

"You're speaking to him."

After falling off his chair, contemplating how he was going to explain this to his wife, he nervously proceeded. "My name is John Gillespie. My wife and I have a desire to start a boys ranch. We heard that you and Cherry may have the same interest. Is that true?"

"Yes, it is," replied the star quarterback.

Boldly he continued, "Is it possible for us to meet with you sometime to discuss this?"

"Sure."

"How would I make an appointment?"

"Well, first, you have to ask for one."

"I'd like to make an appointment."

"Great! Do you want to come over right now?"

Their conversation would continue within a short period of time on the same day. After getting directions from Bart to get to their home, the Gillespies set out to visit the Starrs to discuss the intersecting of Godly visions.

They arrived at the Starrs' modest, three bedroom ranch home. Bart met them at the door and led them into the kitchen, where Cherry was making supper.

"I won't make this long because I don't want to mess up your supper plans."

Cherry then threw this forward lateral of love at the Gillespies. "Please, don't make it quick, or you will mess them up because you're having supper with us!"

Gillespie had to feel like he was going to wake up from this dream at any time.

The four ate supper.

John Gillespie began a low key presentation with flip charts showing the location, structure of leadership, game plans, and other information about what they envisioned for the Boys Ranch.

With a grateful grin, Gillespie remembers, "After each page, Cherry would say, 'Bart, that's just what we were talking about. Bart, that's just what we want to do.'"

Halfway through the presentation Bart put his hand in the middle of Gillespie's book, looked over to his wife, and said, "Cherry, please, let's hear what this couple has to say before we tip our hand!" By then John had a good idea that the Starrs would lend their support to this project.

When the presentation ended, Starr looked over to his wife with a nod of approval. Then he turned to the Gillespies and asked, "How can we help?" Gillespie went on to explain that his strength was not in fund raising and asked for Starr's help in putting the capital together.

"We'd be pleased to help you in this effort," said Bart.

A few months later, with plans for the ranch's development well under way, there came a situation of crisis. For the Rawhide dream, it was fourth and long—real long. John explains, "It was November, just months after we met with Bart. The banker called me at five o'clock Thursday afternoon to remind me if we didn't come up with $20,000 in payment by Monday at 5:00 pm, we would lose the money down and the property would go back on the market."

In desperation, Gillespie sat down at his typewriter and typed: "Dear Bart," then left a lot of space and put the word "HELP" in the middle of the page. He signed it: "Urgently Yours, John Gillespie."

Two days later, Cherry Starr opened the letter. She quickly called her husband at practice.

"Bart, you have to come home right after practice and call John Gillespie!"

"What's the matter?"

When Starr got home from practice, he called promptly.

Gillespie explained the situation to him. Bart not only understood, he took massive action.

John relates this story:

"The following day at practice, with Vince Lombardi's permission, Bart began a short plea to his teammates. He began with a brief vision of the impact the program, now known as Rawhide, could make. He invited the Packer players to come to a luncheon on Monday and to bring a businessman with them."

Keep in mind the players weren't making the money that they make now, thus, it was important to bring some investment candidates.

On Monday, the family met under the direction of their leader, Bart Starr. The meal was held at the Left Guard, a restaurant owned by Fred "Fuzzy" Thurston, the starting left guard on the team.

Fuzzy, unselfishly picked up the tab.

The "Glory Days" Packer heroes in attendance were Henry Jordan, Zeke Bratkowski, and Boyd Dowler. Also there were Carroll Dale and Elijah Pitts. Little known Dave Hathcock, from Memphis State, was there, too. Jerry Kramer and Thurston led some power sweeps in the past, but not like the one needed to score that day.

Bart made a low pressure presentation explaining that this project could and would benefit hundreds of boys. He asked, whoever would choose to do so, to leave a check to help in this effort.

The moment of truth arrived.

John expounds, "The players and their guests began to hand Bart checks. One businessman waited till last and asked me if I wouldn't add up the amount of the checks. I did and it came to near $14,000. Without hesitation, he wrote out a check for the remaining $6,000! I couldn't believe it."

That man was Julius Johnson, known to some as J.O. Johnson, an Appleton Building Contractor.

This true story is just like something from out of the movies. It's the type of thing that has been happening around this Packer organization for a long time.

The Gillespies cried, and continue to be humbled at the thought of that November day in 1965. They call it the "$20,000 Function."

Bart Starr completed 57.42% of his passes during his illustrious career with the Packers, but no completion even closely compares with the Rawhide touchdown, thrown at this luncheon in November of 1965. Starr was known to have thrown touchdown strikes to Carroll Dale and Boyd Dowler, but this day it was the team passing to Rawhide for $20,000!

After the ranch came into being, it should be noted an incredible Rawhide God-incidence occurred. Two of the first boys that came to the ranch to be loved, nurtured, and encouraged were John and Jeff. Oh yeah—they had ties to the Packers. You may recognize their last name. It's spelled: L-A-M-B-E-A-U. That's right. You see, they were the grandsons of Packer Founder Curly Lambeau! And as Paul Harvey would say, "And now you know ... the rest of the story."

Family members knowingly, and sometimes even unknowingly are taking care of their own.

Today Rawhide has become one of the leading juvenile rehabilitation programs in the nation, thanks in large part to Bart Starr and some of his friends who decided to back a dream. 50 boys at a time now stay at Rawhide. Young men are referred by juvenile courts throughout the Midwest. Unfortunately, because of limited space, many have to be turned away. There are plans to expand the Ranch so they can help more young men.

At Rawhide Boys Ranch, a large portion of funds needed to be raised each year are generated through the resale of donated cars, boats, and real estate. In 1995, Rawhide received 5,000 tax deductible gifts of vehicles from thousands of generous folks. However, 50% of the funds are raised through other promotions and gifts.

A couple things were apparent with the early Packers. One is they loved to play football. And two, they loved to do their part in giving to the community. And lastly, these early gentle giants were entertaining and touching people in ways beyond what they were even aware of.

Back in the '60s, Chris remembers playing ball with her Dad on the lawn of their Green Bay home. "I recall him saying, 'Chris come here! You gotta see this.'" They watched, with fascination, as their neighbor painted his eave toughs—without a ladder! It was the big and tall Packer tackle Bob Skoronski.

Thirty years ago, maybe you found yourself in the car at a Green Bay stop sign observing a spherical brown spiraling UFO. There was nothing to fear. It was just Packer quarterbacks Bart Starr and Zeke Bratkowski, who lived across the street from each other, throwing the football high above the street to each other!

As a little boy growing up in Green Bay in the '60s, Butch Belongea remembers having a famous neighbor. He'd ask the neighbor boy if his Dad could come out and play with them. He did. It was Willie Wood, the great Packer defensive back, during the "Glory Years".

One more Bart Starr touching tale. Just a few years after his part in the "$20,000 Function," he donated the Corvette he won as Super Bowl MVP, to Rawhide. Dick Sunde, a former Appleton Jaycee, remembers it well. "We would take the car to different locations around the community. We'd take it all over the area, which included Neenah, Menasha, Appleton, and the surrounding cities. I specifically recall parking it in front of Treasure Island Food Store. We gave people a chance to win it with entry blanks."

Sunde says that Starr was a man of utmost integrity. "Bart was sure to tell us that people did not have to buy anything to take a chance at winning the car. He reminded us to make sure people knew they could make contributions only if they choose to do so. I was impressed with his character and integrity."

With the help of the Appleton Jaycees, nearly $40,000 was raised in the raffle for the car. Today, it sits, like new, in a garage in Hortonville, Wisconsin.

Galatians 6:7 says, "As we sow, so also shall we reap." With a leap of faith through the actions of some of the Glory Day Packers, powerful, eternal seeds were sown. And today, thanks to Vince, Bart, and a few of their friends, who just happened to be football players, the boys at Rawhide and many of us as well, continue to reap the harvest of their planting.

The author, ROBERT BROOKS, and the author's wife KIM ROSE.

GEORGE TEAGUE was recently traded to the Atlanta Falcons for future considerations, but while he was in Green Bay, he was very popular. His "Teague's League" softball team raised thousands of dollars for local charities every summer he was a Packer.

Eight

Still Living and Giving
in Green Bay

From Vince Lombardi to Bart Starr, the Glory Days Packers really began to light the fire of giving back to the community in Wisconsin. The torch of benevolence has been passed.

Today, the Green Bay Packers serve as a model of how a sports franchise can entertain, while reaching out to touch the hearts of millions of people. Like a stone thrown in a still lake, the Packers have produced ripples of love with the energy, depth, and momentum of a tidal wave.

We all notice the success of Brett Favre, Reggie White, and Mark Chmura on the field, but their personal sacrifice of time given to work off the field tends to go unnoticed and is sometimes overlooked.

Many members of the Green Bay Packers take the time to speak at schools, visit hospitals, and donate time for fund raisers in their community. These stories are consistent and never ending. At times many of these positive actions are overshadowed by what the player does on the field.

MVP quarterback Brett Favre put his success on the field to work for the Green Bay area by establishing a "Brett Favre Challenge". Favre donated $150 for each touchdown pass he threw, and nine corporations matched his contribution. At the completion of the season, Favre, who threw for 38 touchdowns and ran for three during the regular season and tossed eight post-season TDs, presented The Boys and Girls Club a check for $73,000! A Brett Favre foundation is being established to assist smaller charities which may go unnoticed.

Ken Ruettgers's radio talk show on WORQ is an example of taking time to give back. Ken's book, *Homefield Advantage*, is also a powerful tool for helping parents become role models for their children. With great sacrifice, he took an off-season to write this self-help, spiritually driven vehicle for his family everywhere. He has spent numerous hours speaking in the community about winning the game at home.

When he was with the Packers, cornerback George Teague unselfishly provided Packer tickets to children throughout the community. He usually hand-delivered them. Teague also presented a sports attraction during the summer. Singer Michael Bolton brought his softball team, Bolton's Bombers, to Appleton for a charity softball game versus Teague's League, a group of Green Bay Packers. All the proceeds go to Children's Hospital.

Sean Jones provided 500 turkey dinners on Thanksgiving Day in conjunction with Sam's Club. He has also served as a United Way spokesman. Teammate, linebacker George Koonce, works on behalf of the Children's Hospital of Wisconsin and Athletes for Youth.

On the offensive side of the ball for the green-and-gold, Anthony Morgan, one of the classiest young men you'll ever meet, works with homeless people and abandoned kids. He also plays in charitable basketball games. Guard Aaron Taylor works locally on a Cerebral Palsy telethon and for the American Heart Association.

The team as a whole has done many things and brightened many a gloomy face throughout the years in Wisconsin. After a Milwaukee game in 1994, the team stopped at a Milwaukee hospital to comfort some children. Through the gift of sharing, the guys on the team have learned that you can't keep sunshine from yourself, while you are sharing it with others. It also helped to keep the players thoughts in perspective. Bryce Paup remembers.

"When you have just lost a football game, you can get pretty ugly and sometimes pretty ungrateful and lose yourself for a bit. But when you go and see some little kids in a hospital suffering, you see what's really important."

More current testimonies of Packer love and sharing are touching and encouraging as well.

Star running back Edgar Bennett has a smile that won't quit, and he uses it and his time as a spokesman for Big Brothers, an organization that provides role models for young boys. He also started a nursing home in his hometown of Jacksonville, Florida, and works with the Mount Bethel Baptist Church there in various events.

Robert Brooks can be found giving a good share of his time to speaking to young people in schools in Green Bay or his home town in South Carolina. Another "Lambeau leaper," LeRoy Butler works with the Fellowship of Christian Athletes in Wisconsin. PAL (Police Athletic League), an underprivileged kids organization, gets his attention at his home in Jacksonville, Florida, in the off-season.

Mark Chmura, the handsome Packer Pro Bowl tight end, works locally with Children's Hospital of Wisconsin. He can also be found out and about quite often showing his appreciation and support for the fans.

One of the tough parts of football for the fans and the players is the business side, especially free agency. Before Ty Detmer, a former Heisman Trophy winner, bolted the Packers to the Philadelphia Eagles after the '95 season, he made his impact in Green Bay. Voted 1995 Packer True Value Man of the Year, he gladly handed his $5,000 check over to the Freedom House of Green Bay. The greatest pass Detmer ever made. The ministry of benefit, under the inspired leadership of Al Bjarnarson, takes care of families in need, helping teenagers and unwed mothers. They provide food, shelter, and love in their Green Bay homes that they prayerfully operate.

Packers Gilbert Brown and Travis Jervey have spent some of their time teaming up for Cystic Fibrosis while allowing fans to have their pictures taken with them.

It's not just the guys who collect grass stains and mud on their uniforms on selected Sundays who are out on the giving trail. Kent Johnston, the Packers strength and conditioning coach, hits the road with a rotating base of 20 Packers to play 25 charity basketball games. In association with community organizations, they help to raise funds for a wide variety of folks. They include everything from the local fire department to the University of Wisconsin-Green Bay Phoenix Athletic Department.

Reggie White is a great football player, but this is pale in comparison to his love for people and his yearning to pass along his message of faith, through Jesus Christ, his Lord and Savior. When White is not chasing quarterbacks, he can be found on street corners sharing his message of hope and faith and educating youngsters about the dangers of drugs, alcohol, and the importance of staying in school. You can't rank any of White's great deeds, and there have been many, but the following may be as good as it gets. It's definitely a "Packer Kleenex-reacher."

In December of 1995, Richard Boelter of Neenah was dying of cancer. His son Richard, Jr., contacted White to tell him about his father, who was failing rapidly from the ravages of leukemia. Boelter's father had a bone marrow transplant and a barrage of chemotherapy sessions. "I called Reggie because Dad was a big fan of his and watched the Packers every week." On December 29, 1995, while the Packers were at a crucial juncture in the season, White returned the call. "Reggie read Scripture to my dad over the phone. They prayed together. My dad told Reggie, 'I'm going to stay here and give you the strength to beat the 49ers.'"

That weekend, the Packers beat Atlanta, 37-20, in Green Bay.

This set up the Packer-49er showdown that Mr. Boelter pledged his help to White to win. Boelter clung courageously to his life.

On Saturday, January 6, Packer game day arrived. The 3:00 p.m. game began. Mr. Boelter, too weak to watch the game on TV, lay with his eyes closed. He listened intently to the play-by-play from his son and family. His pain was covered with joy as the Packers beat San Francisco, 27-17, in one of the great Green Bay games of all time.

Just as he said he would, he persevered and prayed for White and the Packers. As if his mission were accomplished, he died peacefully, 45 minutes after the game. An inspiring end to Boelter's life, thanks in no small part to all-pro defensive end Reggie White. As wonderful as that story is, the rest of the story is even more touching. With Reggie's love and guidance and the leading of the Holy Spirit, Mr. Boelter found and accepted the Lord Jesus Christ as his Savior. He had the confident assurance that when he died he would go to heaven to be with the Lord.

It's easy to get caught up in what a great football player Reggie White is, but the truth is he is a great man that just happens to be a football player.

And so it seems over the years many Packers from Cub Buck to Don

Hutson to Tony Canadeo to Bart Starr to Larry McCarren to Reggie White and many, many others know in their hearts, although they may never have heard the words with their ears, the lyrics to James Taylor's 1970s song, *You've Got A Friend*. In it, Taylor says: "Winter, spring, summer, or fall, all you have to do is call, and I'll be there, yes I will, you've got a friend."

Certain things in this series of events called life are bigger than wins and losses. Being there when your friends need you is certainly is one of them.

Some special people in Green Bay? You know it. And we can tell you that—without question—they are a part of the family. The Packers, like the Energizer Bunny, keep on going and giving. They've even taken timeout from there service to the community to play a few football games. Imagine that!

KEN RUETTGERS had a little fun on Halloween night 1994 when the Packers buried the Bears in a driving rainstorm.

The
Accountability
Group

T he radio listeners in Green Bay are truly lucky—very lucky. The "Timeout" program on WORQ 90.1 FM is one of a kind. The program is a Christian-based talk show that hears the view of many of the players on the Packers. It airs on Monday evenings, from 6:00-7:00 p.m.

Over the last few years, Ken Ruettgers, has unselfishly given one of his greatest resources—his time—to be the key host for the show, while I have been privileged to be the co-host.

Ken Ruettgers believes that not putting a bushel basket over your faith is something he needs to do. "Admitting where you stand spiritually is important. Oftentimes players don't open up about their faith and convictions because nowadays, no matter how big a part your faith plays in their lives, it's just not politically correct to bring it up."

He expounds on the thought. "Part of what I enjoy the most about the show is that it gives my teammates who come on as guests a chance to open up and share who they are. And because it's a Christian radio station, the guys feel a lot freer to reveal that part of their lives because they're not quite as guarded. At a speaking engagement or a business luncheon, it's taboo to talk about your faith," he concluded.

Sean Jones feels compelled to create an awareness of God while competing. "It's important for people to see athletes bowing down giving credit to God in a public forum. Then maybe people will say, 'Hey, it's okay to do that, it's okay to give thanks to the Lord."

A wide variety of testimonies have been heard during the show. From Reggie White to Lenny McGill, personalities, stories, and personal backgrounds vary substantially. From the innocence of an Iowa farm boy named Bryce Paup to the gangs in the street, where Charles Jordan had passed his time till just a few years ago.

It's no surprise Reggie White is the spiritual leader on the Packers. Himself an ordained minister in both the Baptist church he belonged to in his youth and his church in Tennessee, White, along with Ken Ruettgers, form the nucleus for Packer spiritual and team leadership.

In an effort to lead by example, White and Ruettgers assembled between 15 and 20 of their teammates for an accountability group. These gentlemen study the Bible and other Christian books for men. They are not perfect, just forgiven.

Here are some serious and fun moments shared from interviews during the "Timeout" program over the last couple years on WORQ, with Ken Ruettgers and myself.

JOHNNY HOLLAND goes after Dave Krieg of the Lions.

1 - JOHNNY HOLLAND

I f I could have hand-picked my first guest for the radio show, I would have picked Johnny Holland, and he was just that. By the time I met Holland he was retired as a player and had become an assitant coach with the Packers. The former linebacker wore #50 from 1987-1993. A serious neck injury pushed him to retire. He was known as "Mr. Anywhere" for his ability to be where the ball was.

Holland was drafted in 1987 out of Texas A & M. Although he spent some time in Texas, I didn't hear even a hint of an accent. He sported his flat-top haircut, reminiscent of actress Grace Jones, and a goatee. Dressed in a light blue long-sleeve denim shirt, the genial Texan answered all questions directed to him with class.

I remember saying to Holland, "Johnny, I used to wonder what it was about you, why you're such a class act. Now I know. Christ is at the helm of your ship." We talked about what it was like for him to play in Green Bay.

After the show, he was off to the golf course for a celebrity tournament, which brought him here from his home in Texas.

"Johnny, can I get an autograph for my niece and nephew?"

"Sure."

He capped his signature his favorite Bible verse. It's from Philippians 4:13 that says, "I can do all things in him, who stengtheneth me."

He gave me a hug and thanked me for having him on the program. Down the hall he went headed for the golf course.

Today, Johnny Holland is a defensive assistant-quality control coach for the Packers. He had been in business in Sugarland, Texas.

GEORGE KOONCE sets to attack an opposing offense.

2 - GEORGE KOONCE

T|he soft-spoken George Koonce is a two-time guest of the "Time-out" program.

In 1994, during his first appearance, he wore a plaid shirt, jeans, and boots. He looked a lot different than when he wore his number 53 jersey on the field. I was fascinated with how Koonce's neck started just below his ears and broadened until it reached his shoulders. Kind of like a bull or buffalo; totally musclebound. It looked like if he sneezed he'd blow up!

Like Reggie White, George told us he spent some time in the pro football minor leagues. He played in the World League of American Football for the Ohio Glory. It was good practice for him.

His eyes, the window to his soul, showed great care, concern, and sincerity as he answered questions from both Ruettgers and myself. He was quick to give praise to the Lord for all his accomplishments.

"George, where did you go to college?"

"I went to college at a junior college in Murfreesboro, North Carolina. From there I spent two years at East Carolina."

He was a fun interview. Very open.

It was just as much fun interviewing Koonce during the exciting 1995 season. He was very positive about the Packers' chance to win the Super Bowl.

After the program, as he signed my shirt, I asked, "George, what do you eat to stay in shape?"

"Lots of chicken."

"You look healthy, brother," I said.

"Thanks. Gotta go."

He was headed down the hall within seconds.

Ken yelled, "See ya, Georgy."

George Koonce in two words: appreciative, friendly.

STERLING SHARPE always picked up extra baggage after catching passes for the Packers. In this case, he had to lug a Tampa Bay Buccaneer with him on his way to a first down.

3 - STERLING SHARPE

I just about dropped my silver filled teeth the morning Ken told me who our guest was going to be.

Ken, as usual, set the coffee down near our microphones. He pulled a piece of paper out of his wallet. It was always the phone number of the guest. Our first year, the show was at 7:00 a.m., and it was customary for Ken to give his complimentary "wake-up" call to the guest.

I was cuing up a CD when I asked Ken, "Who's coming in?"

With his back to me, heading out of the studio to the nearest phone, Ruettgers casually said, "Sterling Sharpe."

He disappeared around the corner.

"Great," I thought to myself.

Then, like a cross between a heart attack and a bolt of lightning, it hit me. I thought to myself, Wait a minute, this is the guy that doesn't talk to the media! This is the guy who doesn't do interviews! What's special about this show? I wanted to know why he had decided to come in.

Ken came back into the room. "Can he make it in?" I asked.

"He'll be here at about 7:30."

We were short on time before the show and I really didn't have the opportunity nor the time to dwell on what was going to happen over the next hour.

Ken and I talked about the 17-16 loss to New England two days before. I tried with all my being to stay focused, but couldn't help anticipating Sharpe's entrance.

About 7:25, right in the middle of a question to Ken, in walked a handsome, physically fit gentlemen. He was wearing an impressive Nike sweat suit. He was wearing a Packer hat. It was him.

I struggled to keep my composure as Ken motioned to Sharpe to sit next to him at Microphone C. All the while Kenny never missed a beat in our conversation.

"Hey, we have a very special guest this morning, please welcome Sterling Sharpe to the "Timeout" program," Ruettgers said. "Sterling welcome."

"Ken, it's great to be here."

I think the thing that surprised me first was how cool and comfortable Sharpe looked. It wasn't like he did this sort of thing everyday. It spoke a great testament of Ken's solid relationship of trust with him. That's why he had come in. Even still, I recall, how natural this all looked to Sharpe.

Ken continued to ask him questions. All the while I knew my chance was going to come to talk with him—on the radio! I remember thinking as I stared at the talented wide receiver, Man, he's probably one of the top 10 most recognized people in all of sports in America.

It didn't dawn on me at the time this may have been the only radio interview he's ever done while he was in Green Bay. He had premeditatedly avoided the media. It's a story he would share with me a little later.

It was a good thing there had been no pre-promotion of Sharpe's appearance. The parking lot would have become like halftime in the men's room at Lambeau Field.

My chance to talk with Sharpe, after Ruettgers formally introduced Sharpe to me, finally came. I asked Sharpe how he liked Green Bay, about his relationship with other players, and what he thought the chances were of the Pack making it to the Super Bowl.

He explained that he liked Green Bay; however, he was here to play football, not be popular. The guys here, like Ken Ruettgers, he said, are great. He thought the team had a real good shot at making it to the Super Bowl because of the addition of Reggie White, and the emergence of Brett Favre.

As the historic interview proceeded, I remember fumbling with the cassette recorder to the left of the broadcast console. I was trying desperately and unsuccessfully to get it to record. A bit unfamiliar with the set-up, and being a self-proclaimed broadcast equipment illiterate, I failed to get the show on tape. What a loss. If we had, I know the question I asked Sterling Sharpe may have been heard round the world shortly after.

Here's what I asked the talented Packer receiver. "Sterling, if your career came to an abrupt end because of an injury, do you think you could deal with that?"

Sitting very quietly, he responded with words that waffled from humble and modest to downright arrogant, "Yeah, I think so. If God would have my career come to an end, I believe that I could deal with that."

Looking back now, I wonder whether the question actually came from me or from — well, you know.

Little did he, we, or the radio audience know that within just weeks Sterling Sharpe would find out whether he could deal with his career being halted by an injury. Merely weeks after the interview, Sharpe collapsed like a bag of potatoes on the field. Ultimately, it brought an end to his career with the Packers.

As our conversation continued, Sterling talked about his growing relationship with God and about how much he was enjoying the Packer Bible Accountability Group, a weekly gathering of Christians on the team who met for support and fellowship and prayer.

We took telephone calls from the stunned radio listeners and wrapped up the show.

Off the air, Sharpe sat motionless looking straight ahead and commenting on the one point loss to the Patriots two days prior. "I haven't been in the special teams meeting. With the missed PAT (Point After Touchdown) and our kickoff going out of bounds, it just seems like it wasn't to be."

In those precious minutes alone with Ken Ruettgers and Sharpe after the show in the quiet studios, I learned a few things about Sterling Sharpe I'd never known before.

Now very comfortable with Sharpe, and he with me, I boldly asked him, "Sterling, why don't you talk to the media?"

Here's what he said. "Too many times, the media knows the slant they want to take in their stories. I feel they are looking for you to say a couple words that might support their angle and position. Then, they twist some things, and it can change the true story."

Ken Ruettgers concurred.

I really appreciated his honesty and forthright candidness about the issue that had been haunting him in Green Bay since 1988.

Sharpe went on to explain that a Wisconsin paper had misquoted him in his early years as a Packer, and it hurt him—badly. Ever since that time, he had been very uncomfortable about addressing the media. Now, like from Paul Harvey, I had heard the "rest of the story."

Sharpe wasn't through. He commented on something else that had brought out some resentment from the fans in Green Bay. "As far as the autographs; if I sign one, I have to sign a thousand, so I choose to not get involved in it." It brought his comments earlier—about not worrying about being popular—to light.

Was Sharpe just selfish or did he have a point?

If Sharpe didn't want any attention or to be bothered, why did he drive a beautiful, white car with license plates that read: STERL 84?

Early in my relationship with Ken, he confided in me, "If you have 10 people who want an autograph and you only have time to sign eight, you hurt the two more than you brought joy to the others." It did give credence to Sharpe's viewpoint.

Fifteen minutes later, we wrapped it up. Ken had to run to take his son Matthew to school. I nearly had the guts to ask Sharpe for his autograph. I believe he would have given it to me, but I didn't want to take advantage of the situation, or put him in an uncomfortable position, so I didn't.

Sharpe reached out his huge hand, with his trademark, bright, smile, grabbed my hand and gave me a firm handshake. It left me no doubt as to how he could hang on to the football so well. It was the strongest and one of the largest hands I've ever shaken.

After Sharpe left the studios, I couldn't help, but still wonder what it was about this show that was non-threatening. Why had he shown up? He knew that as fellow Christians we wouldn't back him into a corner. I don't think we did.

To this day I ask myself, Did I jinx Sharpe by asking the question about a career ending injury? I don't know, but Ken Ruettgers has jokingly and politely asked me not to ask such a question of him. (I'm not going to.)

Here are some interesting questions I can't help proposing for you to ponder that have come to mind regarding Sterling Sharpe, since he's been gone from the Packers.

Had Sharpe been more accessible to the media, signed autographs, and made himself more available, in general, would he have been given a better sendoff out of Green Bay when he got hurt? Or did the Packer management remember the midnight hour contract debate the day before the 1994 opener?

If this had been the Milwaukee Brewers, and this might have been Robin Yount, Jim Gantner, or Paul Molitor, would the sendoff have been the same?

It's no secret the Packer organization offered Sharpe a few hundred thousand dollars to take the 1995 season off and wait out the situation. It was an attempt to mutually come up with a plan to see if Sharpe may be able to continue his career later. The dollars offered weren't what the receiver thought was fair. It was, comparatively, a mere pittance to the couple million dollars per year contract he had been operating under with the team.

Sterling Sharpe made a decision to end his association with the Green Bay Packers. End of story.

I still get goose bumps, and feel a warm rush, when I remember my brush with greatness that day. It nearly rivals the sick feeling I get when I think about *NOT* getting the treasured minutes on tape. Somewhere out in the radio ionosphere, the words are traveling around the world. The memory *WILL* live forever, in my mind, and those of the listeners, the day Sterling Sharpe talked and took us all for a ride of the radio waves of 90.1-FM, WORQ, in Green Bay.

SEAN JONES is the quintessential NFL player. He's big; he's strong; he's quick; and he's brilliant. In fact, he's smarter than many offensive linemen or he wouldn't have so many quarterback sacks in his career.

4 - SEAN JONES

Man, has this guy got a physique!
That's the first thing that came to my mind as I stared at Sean Jones, the Packer defensive end. Charles Atlas would look like a wimp standing next to him. I'll bet when Atlas set out to find that bully on the beach and started pumping iron, it was Jones he wanted to look like.

Born in Kingston, Jamaica, Jones probably roamed a few warm beaches himself. Today, he is number 96 on the Packers.

One of the first things you learn about Sean Jones is he is very bright. He takes a lap-top computer to work with him. After terrorizing quarterbacks during the season, he is a stock broker in the off season.

Sean's NFL career began in 1984 with the Los Angeles Raiders. From there he went to the Oilers, and now the Pack.

An interesting tidbit of information shows that Reggie White and Jones were born exactly one year apart. Reggie on December 19, 1961, while Jones came into the world on December 19, 1962. Even though Jones has more NFL experience, he is younger than White.

Ken played up Sean real big, then brought him into our conversation. "Hey, Sean, welcome."

"Thanks for having me. How you guys doing?" he said. Sean Jones is the only person I've ever interviewed with a toothpick in his mouth. Not a real easy thing to do, talk with a toothpick in your mouth!

Ken asked Sean, "What do you think about Green Bay?"

"The first thing about changing teams is adjusting to your new teammates, and they are a great group of people here. Secondly, you wonder what kind of adjustments will your family have to make. This community has just embraced us. We've had no problems, it's just been great," he finished.

Jones, the proud papa to be, told us that his wife Tina was due to have a baby on January 1, 1995. She was getting so big, doctors felt they might have to take the baby early.

Ruettgers strategically interjected, "Do you know whether it's …?"

"Yeah, it's a boy!"

Ken added, apologetically, with a smile in his voice, "I'm sorry, that wasn't politically correct was it?"

We burst out laughing.

"The doctors said if she goes fullterm, the baby will be about eleven pounds, and I don't want to subject my wife to that!" Jones replied. "If they take him a couple weeks early, he may be around eight pounds."

Then, very seriously Jones said, "I tell you what, when you have a pregnant wife, and I presume there are a few people out there in the listening audience who do, it changes your whole perspective on life. I always pray that I can be a good husband to my wife. When you see your wife going through that, I kid her and say 'It looks like you swallowed a beach ball.' It really is a blessing for us."

The conversation took a tone and turn of direction when Ruettgers said, "Isn't it something how when you are going to be a dad, you are more tuned in to the issues, the things that will affect your children?"

"Exactly. The things that will affect my child, like school system, crime, and quality of life. Now I realize that in months they will directly impact my little guy."

Sean Jones brought up a great point when he added, "It doesn't bother me so much when I see things going on, but what really bothers me is that we're not doing anything about them, so it's made me more aware of how these things can affect me personally."

Ironically, it was election day (November 4, 1994), and we talked about how not enough people get out and vote on the issues.

Jones noted, "Only 30% of the people will get out and vote today. That's ludicrous. People won't vote, and then later they'll complain their guy didn't win."

For a portion of the program we talked about the importance of Christians to be good examples and role models, but we also made it clear that Christians aren't perfect. I loved what Jones said, "Christians are all sinners in recovery; however, anyone can choose to be cleansed and forgiven by Christ's blood."

We went to the telephone line. I said, "Jeff, you're on with Sean Jones and Ken Ruettgers."

"How you guys doing?"

"Great. How are you?" the twin towers, echoed.

Jeff directed his question to Sean. "My wife has a problem with Christian athletes getting together and praying on the 50 yard line after games because of the violent nature of the game."

"Well, here's the way we look at it. When we are on the field, playing hard, we are bouncing around on each other, but after it's over, it's over. We are just doing are job."

Ken expounded, "You know, it's a game, it has rules and risks. The Lord gives us the ability to compete and glorify him, and Christian football players are going out to try to do just that. It is the closest thing to 'peacetime war.' But that's part of the game, part of the allure, the man on man, one on one, the best against the best."

Ken continued, "I can see on the surface why someone may have a problem with that. They may think it's hypocritical to be a Christian and a football player, but when you really break it down, we're just doing our jobs."

I asked Sean about Green Bay fans.

He replied, "The Green Bay fans are very supportive here. They are not very 'front-runningish', if there is such a word. There's more of a comradery between the fans and the players here. Even when we don't do as well on the field, as they'd like, I know the fans are still behind us."

Jones then gave a dose of what it was like elsewhere. "In Houston, I think there was too much apathy there. If you won games, they shut up; if you lost games, they were nowhere to be found."

Ken Ruettgers had a question that he always wanted to ask Jones. "Sean, what is it that you love so much about football?"

"In football, no matter what your record, every time the ball is snapped there is a challenge, a chess match going on, and that's what I love about it. Trying to make the right moves. The other day I prayed the play before and got a sack!"

Things lightened up considerably when I said, "Sean, you played against the Packers in 1993 in the Houston. (Green Bay won, 16-14) You and Ken Ruettgers went head to head, hand to hand that night. He was telling me before you came in that all he remembers is seeing the Astrodome ceiling as you bowled him over!"

They both laughed. Sean acknowledged that it wasn't that way at all. He went further. "I believe Ken Ruettgers is in the top four of all offensive tackles in the NFL."

I jokingly asked Jones, "Hey, which show was more fun, this one or Roy Firestone's "Up Close"? The previous week during the Packer bye week he'd flown to California to appear on the ESPN program.

He got a kick out of that.

I wrapped it up by saying a good finish to the season would be to win the rest of their games, win the Super Bowl, and then have the Lord come back! They both roared their approval.

I told Kenny to hand Jones his parting gift for being on the show. It was a dry Hardee's Danish. It was one we hadn't gotten around to eating yet.

In 1995, Sean appeared again. That night Charles Jordan came in along with Jones to co-host with me as Ken took his sweetheart out of town during the bye weekend. Charles was entertaining as usual, and Sean was having fun. Jones humbly pointed out that he had graduated from Northeastern when he was only 20. With Ken gone, I couldn't resist taking a jab at my absent friend. "I heard that Ken Ruettgers took, like, eight years to get through USC. I think he was 26, or something!"

Jones said, "Ken talks about his Masters. Maybe they just gave it to him."

With friends like Jones and myself, Ruettgers certainly doesn't need enemies. It was all in fun.

Seriously, I asked Sean, "What's the greatest thing about Ken Ruettgers?" I loved his answer.

"All the things that are great about Ken have nothing to do with football. He is a man of character, integrity, and he makes his family priority, right behind the Lord."

Later in the show, both Charles Jordan and Jones joked that Packer players needed to boycott the team barber, Robert Brooks. "His prices are getting a little high," Jones teased. It never dawned on me that it may be tough for an African-American man to get a haircut in Green Bay. I was getting a little lesson on culture during this interview.

Jones thought it unusual that in Green Bay you can't take your small children into the movie theater. He seemed a bit frustrated by that.

Both Jones and Jordan politely acknowledged—without words—that Green Bay isn't quite Houston or L.A., when it comes to selection of restaurants. "If you're looking for a good 'Cajun' meal, you may be looking for a while, but there are a lot of great places here in Green Bay, too," he confessed.

I thanked both the guys for coming in on the night before their day off. They said they had fun.

Jordan hugged me and left. He had some plans.

I walked with Jones to the other room and had him sign a football and a couple shirts. I asked him, "Why do you always wear long sleeves on the field, no matter whether it's hot or cold?"

He said, "Just a habit. It's something I've always done, so I just keep doing it."

I then learned this wasn't his only idiosyncrasy. He also is sure to be the last player off the field in pre-game warmups.

Sean Jones is a big, strong man, but his body is not nearly as strong and solid as his character, confidence, and conviction to professional standards and values.

Oh, by the way. Little Dylan Jones was brought into the world on December 15, 1994, two weeks before Tina's due date, just like Sean said he might. Today, Dad, Mom, and baby are fine.

CHARLES JORDAN did a fine job as a wide receiver when he was with the Packers.

5 - CHARLES JORDAN

I hit it off with Charles Jordan from the moment he sat down at our microphone in 1994. He returned to co-host a "Timeout" program with Sean Jones in 1995.

Jordan wore number 80 during his two seasons with the Packers. Every time I saw Charles I brought up the nationally televised pre-season game in 1994. Jordan, at the time, was a free agent with the Raiders and was struggling to make the team. With time running out on him and in the game with his team behind, he made a circus catch jumping over the back of an Oiler defensive back to score a game-winning touchdown.

Jordan had really arrived in the NFL through the back door. After spending just one year in college at Long Beach Community College, he gave up on football. It wasn't a smart choice. After he saw the light, the Los Angeles Raiders gave him a second chance at football.

On the program, Jordan explained. "I didn't have any videotape of myself, but I sent a letter to the Raiders. They called me and asked, 'Do you really run a four two (4.2 seconds) in the forty yard dash?' I said I did, so they invited me in for a tryout. It worked out."

In 1993, Charles chewed on the Packers in a pre-season game in Canton, Ohio. It was the Hall of Fame Game, in which the Raiders blistered the Packers in the summer sun, 19-3.

Along with Ken Ruettgers and me, Jordan told the 1994 "Timeout" crowd, "I think ever since Ron Wolf saw me in that game, he was looking for my name on the waiver wire." The waiver list includes those players who have lost jobs (fired) with NFL teams. They are free to be signed by other teams. Wolf couldn't wait till this happened; he traded for Jordan the week before the 1994 campaign.

Charles is a huggable, gentle spirited young man. As he told the story of his life, you couldn't believe he had been part of such a mess. Life hadn't been all glitz and glory for Jordan. On this day he looked pretty happy, content, and peaceful. Just years before, Jordan explained he'd been involved in gang activity and other sin in L.A., where he grew up.

He didn't get real graphic, but we read newspapers and watch TV to give us an idea.

Actually, Charles had been on the straight and narrow for much of his life. He explained. "I accepted the Lord into my heart in 1976 when I was in 4th grade, then I rededicated my life while with the Raiders." Charles is a walking testimony that God can make a person new.

Sean Jones said during his appearance along with Jordan on the show, "I think Charles should write a book called, *From Gangster to Gridiron*. We laughed; but you know, he should.

It was interesting during the 1994 show as Jordan talked about the many L.A. Raider players baptized in the team Jacuzzi! Big, macho guys who play pro football, surrendering themselves to God. Being dunked in the tank of living water.

"Vince Evans and Jeff Hostetler baptized 27 or 28 people," he said.

"Vince Evans is nearly as old as John the Baptist!" I quipped. That drew a good laugh from both Ruettgers and Jordan.

Minutes later, I looked at the diminutive Jordan and laughed, "Charles, you're tiny! I'd think when those guys hit you on punt returns, your arms and legs would fly off. How do you survive?"

"After some plays, you're kinda dizzy, and after the game you sit in some ice, but it's not too bad," he smiled.

"How big are you anyway?"

"Five ten—and a quarter," he said with an emphasis on the quarter. He wanted people to know he was bigger than just 5'10".

Jordan stressed the fact that it is more important for pro athletes to give their time rather than just money to kids' causes in the community. Jordan said his passion is to help the young children realize that gangs, drugs, and trouble aren't cool. "I want kids to know that the streets bring a dead end. If they need to talk to anybody, they can talk to me."

It broke my heart when I read the Packers decided after the 1995 season not to match Jordan's free agent offer from the Miami Dolphins. Along with thousands of fans, we wish him well. Charles Jordan made an impact through his love and choice to bless those around him in Green Bay.

6 - PEPPER BURRUSS

epper Burruss made his first visit to the "Timeout" program in November of 1995. He returned to bless us in September of 1996 as well.

During the first season of the radio show, Ken and I would take the first half hour to talk about stuff, then the guest would come in. This was the case the first time Burruss came in. We took a commercial break, and Ken introduced me to Pepper.

Back on the air, Ken told the audience, "Folks, it's my pleasure to welcome the head trainer of the Packers, Pepper Burruss, to the 'Time-out' program."

"Thanks, Kenny, it's great to be here."

We skipped the small talk. I got right to the meat. "Pepper, where were you working before you came to the Packers?"

"Before coming to Green Bay, I served 16 years as trainer for the New York Jets," he answered smoothly. I was floored. Pepper has a real youthful look about him. I couldn't imagine he had been in the NFL that long. Looking much younger than his 40 years, Burruss acknowledged he had just recently suffered his "milestone" birthday.

As a trainer, Burruss winds miles and miles of tape around ankles, and he watches over the bumps and bruises. He's quite a servant. He's learned from the Greatest.

"Back in the spring of 1977, I asked Christ to be the center of my life. Shortly after, I got the phone call that offered me my first job out of school to be the assistant trainer with the New York Jets."

As we continued with the Packer trainer, he told us that one of the scary things about the game of football is the injuries. Unfortunately, Burruss has seen his share.

In the history of the radio program I can't recall a more dramatic story as the one Burruss told about the New York Jets' Dennis Byrd. Burruss was there—up close—for the Dennis Byrd nightmare in November of 1992. Byrd was a defensive end for the Jets. During a play attempting to sack a quarterback, he slammed his head and neck into a teammate. Instantly, his body went limp.

Burruss remembered the details like it were yesterday.

"When two guys would get injured on the same play, Bob Reese (of the Jets) and myself would go out on the field and each attend to a player. As fate would have it, I went to Dennis Byrd.

"'Peppy, I can't move my legs, I broke my neck.'"

Burruss said in a blanket statement, "Okay." He was implying that they would take care of him.

After he was carted off the field, his wife Angela joined them. Pepper recalls there were exchanges of "I love you," and he remembers this chilling comment that Byrd made to his wife. "I just want to be able to hold you and Ashton." Ashton is his little girl.

"I couldn't help but think about the possibility of having held my son for the last time, so that sent chills through me" said Burruss somberly.

Byrd was loaded into an ambulance for the trip to a Manhattan hospital. Along with Byrd were his wife, New York Jets physician, Dr. Steve Nicholaus, and Burruss.

Burruss recalls the incredible drama that unfolded during the trip. "We were about 10 minutes away from Giants Stadium, where we had literally peeled Dennis off the turf. The sirens were blaring, and we were praying out loud in a conversational tone. Here it was, the scariest moment of his life, and he is raising his hand to the ceiling of the ambulance thanking his Lord and Savior, Jesus Christ, for trusting him with this injury, knowing that he was strong enough to stand up under this trial."

Burruss planted his eyes into Ken's and commented, "You talk about things that shake your faith, it took my breath away. It was as if time stood still. I had to ask myself, Could I have said that—oh, ye of little faith? It made the hair on the back of my neck stand up."

Ours did too.

The story has a happy ending.

"I saw Dennis speak a few months ago in front of about 4,000 people as he delivered the keynote address for the National Athletics Trainers Association.. He has learned to walk and is making strides. He just overwhelmed the crowd with his story."

Pepper told of some of the ribbing he took as one of the TV networks aired, *The Dennis Byrd Story*. Kenny asked Pepper, "Did you know who was going to play you in the movie?"

Without cracking a smile he said, "I thought it would either be Mel Gibson or Tom Cruise, they both have legs like mine."

Ruettgers and I lost it.

His role was played by Richie Allen, a man in his 50s, and 50 to 60 pounds heavier than Burruss.

"A couple minutes into the network TV movie, even with call waiting, I had three calls. 'Hey Pepper, a few gray hairs, huh? Hey Pepper, a few extra pounds, eh?'"

Allen was actually the plop, plop, fizz, fizz, guy in the old Alka Seltzer commercials. Pepper dished a little out and can take it as well.

I asked Burruss, "Tell us some of the tough guys on the Packers and some of the wimps."

"Well, one of the cream puffs is sitting next to me."

He was talking about Ken, of course.

The big tackle smirked, sat up straight at attention in his chair, and listened closely to Pepper's accusations. Burruss told how Ruettgers would sit reading the paper in the Packer training room and yell for Pepper to come attend to some of his aches and pains. "I was thinking of getting Kenny a little bell that he could ring when he needed me."

"Am I spoiled or what?" confessed Ruettgers.

Ken never blushed a bit. He did crack a little smile and took it all in stride.

It got better.

I added, "Ken, I bet you're pampered at home with Sheryl getting your slippers."

Burruss couldn't resist. "Well, I don't know if I'd say that, but I did drive by the Ruettgers house this morning and saw Sheryl taking out the garbage, shoveling snow, and mowing the lawn! I don't think that's spoiled, I don't have a problem with that," he joked.

I had been prodding Kenny for weeks to bring Sheryl on the program. "Now I'm starting to question whether I should bring her on the show or not," Ruettgers joked. Eventually he did. She was a lot of fun.

Burruss went on to tell of Reggie Miracle #1, during the program, which was in an earlier chapter.

Pepper graced the audience with his presence again in 1995.

I recall Burruss taking a tiny jab about him not being one of the guys making *real money.* "This morning my wife blasted off for Bellin College of Nursing. Somebody has gotta make real money 'cause you know I'm makin' chicken feed." He was teasing.

Burruss pointed out later that money can't buy the incredible experiences and friendships he has earned with some of the players and coaches. He verified the fact that there are hundreds of people who would do what he does for free.

A couple months after the 1994 show I ran into Pepper at McDonalds in Green Bay. He recognized me and treated me like family.

In 1995, Pepper picked up right where he left off. "How appropriate for a trainer to be on a program called 'Timeout'. It's only during breaks that trainers get on the field."

I said, "Pepper, millions of people get to see you, but nobody knows who you are."

He had a solution to advance his cause, not so people would know him, but to advance his cause.

He joked, "The NFL won't let us do it, but I think, like Rocky Balboa's trainer, we should be able to have jackets with advertisements on the back. 'Eat at Sam's Place,' that would be strong."

Tom from Green Bay called in. He was having some struggles in his life, and he said how much he appreciated Ken's honesty about his trials and told Pepper Burruss he had a lot of respect for him, especially after seeing *The Dennis Byrd Story.*

Said Burruss to the caller, "Tom, when I get on my knees next to my son's bed tonight, you'll be in my prayers, bro."

Sounding delighted and a bit honored, Tom said, "Thank you, guys."

One of the downsides to Pepper's work is that he must be the bearer of bad tidings to coaches about injuries.

"Do the coaches get kind of mad at you sometimes," asked Ken.

"Sometimes, but I try to tell the coach that in the Bible they rarely killed the messenger! I try to remind them of that."

Ken kicked Burruss out because our guest had his daughters birthday party to go to. His daughter Christina Marie was two that day.

"It's too bad you guys had to lower yourself to have a trainer on," he quipped as he headed for the door.

Weeks after his 1995 appearance on the "Timeout" program, Burruss was seen by millions again as he attended to Gil Haskell after the play when the Packer receivers coach was decked in Dallas. Robert Brooks and a Dallas defender ran into Haskell on the sidelines. As he did with Byrd, he stayed by his side and helped him through.

All you can say about Pepper Burruss is he is a servant, a true giver with a heart loaded with love and hope. He is a great role model on the Packers, in the community, and to his family, especially little Christina Marie.

I have an incredible sense that God intentionally predestined Pepper Burruss to share in the miracles of Reggie White, as well as the touching stories of Dennis Byrd, Ken Ruettgers, and Gil Haskell. He now serves as a witness of the miracles and uses them to share his hope and faith with others.

LeSHON JOHNSON played sparingly with the Packers before being released in 1995. He was immediately picked up by the Arizona Cardinals. In the spring of 1996, he had laser surgery done to his eyes, and at last reports, he was making a mark in Arizona's training camp.

7 - LeSHON JOHNSON

Good looks, the innocence of a choir boy, and feet as quick as lightning, LeShon Johnson appeared to be perfect for the Green Bay Packers. He wore number 42 during his stay with the Packers in 1994 and half of 1995. I'll always smile when I think of LeShon Johnson. At 23 years old, this charming gentlemen would melt most ladies' hearts within a million mile radius of him. If his innocence couldn't get you, his words would.

It was Tuesday, December 13, 1994, when Johnson made his first appearance on the show. He sat in a pure white, long-sleeve shirt that partially covered a beautiful gold watch that hugged his left wrist. His smile shined like the gel that pulled his jet black hair back.

He brought smiles to Packer fans in 1994, when he'd streak through a hole for a gain. He had great potential. That's a scary word. It proved that way for LeShon. As it turned out, he never reached it in Green Bay.

"Our special guest today is LeShon Johnson. LeShon, welcome to the show," said Ruettgers.

For me, it was his somewhat naive, candid innocence that drew me to Johnson. He was a self-admitted, laid back cowboy, literally. That was his nickname, "Cowboy." He grew up riding broncos in Oklahoma.

"Have you ever been to Reba McIntyre's ranch in Oklahoma?" I asked.

"No."

I think he thought I was serious.

LeShon returned to the show in 1995 season. He shared the funniest, silliest, and most bizarre story we ever heard on the "Timeout" program. His youthful heart shined as he explained how he and fellow running back Travis Jervey had recently ordered out. Not for a pizza, but a pet. Not a cat, dog, snake, or horse, but a lion! A baby African lion!

Coach Holmgren found out about it. As if with a couple of high schoolers, Coach Holmgren addressed the issue with both Johnson and Jervey.

LeShon explained, "He said, you guys *aren't* going to bring a lion up here to Green Bay."

LeShon pleaded, "We'll give it to a zoo or something when it gets older."

"I don't care if you guys sent money or not; if you did, you lost it!" the Coach told them.

So much for that idea.

"Now we were thinking of getting something else, like a monkey or something."

I don't know what the listeners thought, but Ken, I, and our producer Scotty just about fell off our chairs! He was serious. I bet this guy's a riot at a funeral.

When I composed myself, sat up straight, and pointed my lips directly into the microphone and quipped, "In case some of you have just tuned in, this is our weekly program on WORQ called 'Timeout' *and Pet Corner!*"

To this young man's credit, he has a sincere love for people that shows through his commitment to our Lord and Savior, Jesus Christ.

After the show, I told Johnson how much he fit in Green Bay on the field and with the fans. He thanked me, then signed a couple shirts, shook my hand, and left.

Unfortunately, it was the last time I'd see him. Within days, he was cut by the Packers to make room on the roster for Keith Jackson.

I won't forget this young man anytime soon. He touched me. The 5'11", 200-pound speedster had so much to offer the team, in my opinion, but it didn't work out.

I get a little sad when I look at a picture of LeShon, Kenny, and me taken after the '95 show, knowing I'll probably never see Johnson again.

I was thrilled when I found out that the Arizona Cardinals signed him a day after the Packers released him. I'm sure there were a lot of other people happy for him too.

8 - GUY McINTYRE

I was rolling out of bed one morning during the off-season in 1994, when the sportscaster blared through my clock radio, "The Packers have signed 49er great, Guy McIntyre." I pictured his name across his #62 jersey and the neck-roll he wore for San Francisco. Now he was a Packer.

A few months later, Guy's stop on the radio set started with a bang. The night before, McIntyre's former team, the 49ers, had appeared to lie down and let them Vikings beat them. It cost the Packers a Central Division Championship.

Ken Ruettgers began the interview with a ribbing. "What happened on 'Monday Night Football' to your old buddies?"

Guy, who has a tremendously hearty laugh, provided one for us.

"I don't know man."

McIntyre told us he grew up in a village of 15,000 people in the south Georgia town of Thomasville.

"Along with me, there's Charlie Ward, who won the Heisman Trophy, and Julie Moran, from 'Entertainment Tonight', grew up there." he said proudly.

"Can you get some of the water shipped up from there?" echoed Ruettgers.

In the off-season, McIntyre is a tireless volunteer and helps to provide a charity basketball game for the small town.

"Last year Ronnie Lott, Joe Montana, and Sterling Sharpe came and played. This year Ty Detmer says he's gonna play. He says he has a game," Guy said a bit skeptically.

It had been a while since I picked on Ken, so I said, "I heard that you can actually increase your attendance at that stuff if you advertise that Ken Ruettgers will not be playing!" I finished my ribbing with, "They call him 'Slam Dunk Ken'."

"Actually my name is 'Bricks' Ruettgers," Ken said. He's always been able to take teasing very well.

Ken and I were anxious to hear about Guy McIntyre's strong, Christian roots, as well as those of the San Francisco 49ers.

He gave some names of the Christians on his former team. "We had Brent Jones, Steve Wallace, Jesse Sapulu, Merton Hanks, and myself, going to regular Bible study," he acknowledged.

We got a taste of the guts, fermentation, and true aging of McIntyre's spiritual life as we talked about his stay on the Green Bay Packers injured list in 1994. He was out six games with a blood clot, following the opener. He returned to help the Packers slam the Bears in Chicago. Guy shared and showed how his injury was used by God to strengthen his faith.

"It's frustrating, but sometimes God helps us to realize what's really important. At times God has to pull the reins and say slow down. There are times when you're down and all you can do is let Him have it," said McIntyre.

The Packer left guard continued with some incredible insight. "Faith is faithful—God will bring you through. Sometimes we get way ahead of Him and lose patience, and He wants to bring you back to him. We get tied up in games, events, and relationships. Our relationship with God and family need to be first."

Did you know that Guy McIntyre played left tackle and Ken Ruettgers played left guard during one game? Actually, it was for one play during the Bear-Packer clash on "Monday Night Football" in 1994.

McIntyre explains. "I had just pulled a groin muscle on the play before. All of a sudden Coach Holmgren wants to call an 18 Lob. As we were headed out of the huddle and to the line I said, 'Kenny, I can't pull!"

"What do you wanna do?" panicked Ruettgers.

"Switch with me."

"Really?"

"Yeah."

At the last second we flip-flopped. I played tackle, and he played guard, and Ruettgers became the hero," remembered Guy. During that very play, Edgar Bennett ran to the right, Ken made a great block, and Bennett went in for the score.

Although Guy McIntyre spent just one season with the Packers, it was long enough for him and Ruettgers to develop a deep admiration and friendship for each other.

"Guy, tell us about Ken Ruettgers," I asked.

"When we got to Green Bay, Kenny and his wife opened up their hearts and home to us. They kept our dog, they gave us pots and pans, they fed us, they let us use their vehicle. When we first got here, it took a while to get our family situated, and Ken and Sheryl were so helpful."

McIntyre and his wife Michelle have three children.

Guy continued heaping praise upon his fellow lineman. "Ken's a great guy with a great heart. He does what the Lord wants him to do. He's putting some great ideas down on paper. (He was referring to Ken's book, which Ken was still writing.) It's been great working with Ken. The community should also enjoy and appreciate Ken off the field and see what kind of guy her really is."

I asked McIntyre a question I've always wanted to ask a football player. I had never gotten the courage to ask Ken.

"Guy, what's it feel like when the referee throws a flag, then gets on the wireless microphone, and tells 60,000 people, not counting the millions watching on TV, that you just committed a penalty?"

Guy smiled and said, "You feel like you're alone out on an island with a spotlight on you. Like you said, you can do so much good, then the one time you get caught the coaches are yelling, 'What did he do that for?' Everybody knows I wouldn't hold," he said as he let out a big laugh.

Time was running short, but my partner made sure that he said what was on his heart about his teammate.

"I want to make a comment. Guy and I don't always see eye to eye politically and a few other issues."

Ruettgers is a staunch conservative, while McIntyre is a liberal.

Ken continued, "Our common foundation as brothers in the Lord supersedes any difference we may have. We really have fun teasing each other. I respect and try to understand his perspectives. I love Guy because he's a brother in Christ."

Scotty mentioned that we had to wrap it up. I thanked the sponsors, then closed with, "On behalf of Guy McIntyre and Ken Ruettgers, this is Steve Rose, make it a great week everybody," as the theme tailed out.

"And, Guy, don't hit your head on the rim during one of those charity basketball games!"

"No, that's only possible when I'm putting up the net, standing on a ladder."

After his '94 season with Green Bay, Guy McIntyre accepted a new business arrangement with the Philadelphia Eagles. What a guy! No pun intended. I'm very grateful, along with Ken Ruettgers, his Packer teammates, and many fans as well that God brought him to Green Bay, even if for only one season.

BRYCE PAUP has Detroit's Rodney Peete in his grasp.

9 - BRYCE PAUP

I was sitting next to my microphone when I saw Ken coming down the hall in his big, green, winter jacket. He wasn't holding coffee, Danishes, or anything like that. He had a spoon in one hand and a pint of something in the other.

"How's it going, bud?" he said.

"Good, partner. How was your week?" I presumed it went well. He didn't respond, but got right to the issue.

"I brought you some Ben's."

"Ben's" is Ken Ruettgersese for Ben & Jerry's Ice Cream. Since the beginning of my relationship with Ken, we had talked a lot about our mutual love affair—with ice cream. Me, a weakness for Blizzards; for Ken his devotion to the "yuppie" ice cream made in Vermont. He set the delicacy down next to me along with the spoon. "There, now you can try some."

"What kind is it?"

"Chocolate Chip Cookie Dough," he said.

He was proud to have brought me the present, and I was thrilled he did. I didn't waste any time as I dug right in. Talk about "sin by the pint," that stuff was great!

The show started, and like normal clockwork, the guest showed up around half past. He was a fair-skinned man with a little bit of a five o'clock shadow beard, about 6' 4", muscular, and great looking.

We usually took a break as a bumper to allow the guest to get comfortable and to meet me. Bryce Paup and I got along great from the onset.

During the commercials, I slammed a couple tablespoons of Ben & Jerry's. It was almost all melted. It was like thick cream with gobs of unbaked chocolate chip cookie dough.

"Bryce, I'd give you some, but you have the Pro Bowl in a couple weeks."

"Yeah, Bryce," Ken said a little sarcastically, but teasingly.

Paup had been elected to play in the Pro Bowl in Hawaii. The team had just been beaten by Dallas (so what else is new) and the season was over for everyone, but Paup. At the time, Ken planned on going to do some interviews for his book. He later decided not to make the trip.

We took to the airwaves to talk with the man who wore number 95 for the Packers, from 1990 to 1994. "Ladies and gentlemen, meet Bryce Paup. Bryce thanks for coming in," Ken told the audience.

We entered into some small talk, then Ken hit right to the issues.

"Bryce, how tough is it to break the overachiever stereotype?"

"Labels are tough. Back before my rookie year, I didn't run a good time in the 40-yard dash, and I was just looked at as not very talented. It's frustrating."

The fact that Bryce Paup was on his way to Hawaii to the Pro Bowl should have been enough to silence a few of his critics.

After a break, Matthew called. In a frightening bit of irony, he asked this question of Paup. "Is your relationship with your team affected if you sign with another team?"

Paup was an unrestricted free agent when he answered, "Well, basically, you're not going to be there anymore. If I signed somewhere else, I'd still keep in contact with my friends on the team, like Kenny. I'm not going to see him everyday, but I can still talk to them."

Ken helped to draw out a little bit more of Matthew's concern. "Matt, are you wondering about how Bryce's relationship with the players or how they are affected if Bryce doesn't sign back with the Packers or not because of the friends he has on the team?"

"Yeah," he admitted.

Paup responded: "Well, friends are great, but when it comes down to making a business decision you have to do what's best for your family. I'm going to pray a lot about it and go where God wants me to be. If it's it back in Green Bay, I'll be here. If it's not, he'll give me a peace about where I'm supposed to be."

Paup's answer would be easy to accept had God nudged him to stay in Green Bay. Of course, he signed a deal with the Buffalo Bills and went on the become the NFL Defensive Player of the Year in 1995.

Ruettgers, who is tremendously sensitive, made a great point to the young man.

"You know, Matt, because I've been through this before and know what it's like (contract negotiations), Bryce knows that he knows that we know that it's part of the business of football and true friendships will endure and the greatest friendships are those based in the Lord."

Ruettgers wisdom continued, "Some relationships that are just based on football don't endure. Thank God for telephones and the mail so we can keep in touch with our true friends."

Great answer. It doesn't help to take the edge off of the sting of having lost Paup, but it does shed some light on the subject and help fans to understand the reality of football free agency.

I couldn't help but try to cheer everyone up and asked Ken, "Now, God forbid, if Bryce would hold out, but do you still have the pool in Bakersfield, that you sat around when you held out?"

"No, we sold it. We'll have to just send him out to the bay."

We laughed.

We dug into Paup's Iowa roots.

"Now, where did you grow up? In Scranton?"

"Well, I grew up there, but didn't spend much time there. We were in Jefferson a lot."

Having spent some time in Iowa myself in the early '80s, I decided to start on the common ground with the Packer linebacker.

"You know where Clarion is?"

"Right on highway 3."

"Yep, I rescued my wife from the cornfield there," I added.

Paup, who looked much bigger on the field than in person, told of how different it was to go back home in the off-season, work on the family farm, and have people make a fuss over him.

Ken Ruettgers, the California guy, had only seen a picture of a cow or a cornfield, didn't fit in very well in the early part of the interview. Ken looked to be enjoying the conversation as Paup and I talked about soybeans and pigs.

During the last break, the guys got into some conditioning jargon that, frankly, I couldn't understand. My interpretation was that Bryce was going to the Packer training center later in the day to work on some different forms of conditioning.

We went to the telephone one more time, and a young boy named Peter called with a great question.

"Why do some of the players put tape across their nose?"

"It's to help you breathe easier," said Paup. "I was a little skeptical at first until I tried it. It has a little spring in it. You put it across the bridge of your nose and it opens your nasal passages and you can breath easier."

"I tried it and it worked OK for me, but not good enough," Ruettgers acknowledged facetiously, referring to the fact that the Packers didn't beat the Cowboys days before. Ken went a little further. "It really did work, but you know I started sweating and it started to slip off."

"His nose is too small," interrupted Paup, in his only attempt at comedy.

"All right, Jimmy Durante!" Ruettgers told his teammate.

We took another call. This time from Tom. "Ken or Bryce, share a life changing experience that might have taken place that might have gotten you guys on fire."

For two seconds there was silence, Ken went, "Hm-m..." Then simultaneously, both Ruettgers and I blurted out, "Bryce."

Immediately, Ruettgers and I roared with laughter. I had caught that Ken wanted Bryce to answer the question and was going to help him get off the hook.

I looked at Ken with a huge smile, and he gleamed at me and said, "That was good!"

"I handed off to Ken, and Ken jammed the ball to Bryce. Take it up the middle pal," I urged Paup regarding the caller's question.

"Shoot, that kinda put me on the spot. Well, I guess the first one was when I was four years old and I gave my life to Christ," said Paup.

"Why'd you wait so long?" I jabbed with a serious look, but tongue in cheek.

"I'd been struggling for so long," laughed Paup.

After a split second, we all laughed, then he continued somberly.

"That was the first experience and a lot of people say, 'You don't know what you're doing when you're four years old, but I knew exactly what I was doing. There was an alter call given (a chance to accept Christ), and I knew I had to be up there."

Candidly Paup said that it hasn't been exactly a bowl of cherries since then, but God is faithful and is guiding him.

Paup explains. "There are some things about playing football that can be frustrating, but God shows Himself faithful through the valleys and let's you know He's in charge. He let's you know that even though you don't understand it, He has your best interests in mind."

Bryce told of the battles and dilemmas that Christians encounter, the fears and doubts that require complete faith in God.

"I was a little frustrated with the way things went early in my career, and I was having a tough time giving football to God. I had heard so many stories of people giving certain areas of their lives to God, only to have them taken away shortly after."

We all laughed because we knew exactly what he was saying and have all felt the same way at one time or another.

He finished. "Finally I was able to give football to the Lord, and it was then that I made the starting line up and things began to really fall into place."

We had to take one last break. During the commercials, Paup and Ruettgers entered into some conditioning jargon. Like usual, I was baffled.

We returned.

Continuing to listen and watch Bryce, I couldn't believe this guy could go out and crush quarterbacks and Barry Sanders. As I looked at Ken, I realized he wasn't necessarily Godzilla off the field either. I learned these guys can be real pussy cats when they're not working.

"Bryce, what's it like to try to catch Barry Sanders?"

He sighed, "Uhhh ... a helpless feeling."

"Is it like back on the farm trying to catch a greased hog?" I asked.

"That might be a little easier, but God's given him a great pair of feet and if you try to dance with him, he's got the best in the world and if he's 'even, he's leavin'," he said. What he was saying was that if you hadn't gotten your mitts on Sanders by the time he hit the line of scrimmage, where the ball is put in play, he was gone.

You could also assume he meant if you weren't in front of the slick running back, he'd leave you, your spikes, and possibly some other personal equipment lying on the field.

We talked about Emmitt Smith of the Cowboys, another great running back.

"It feels good being able to make an open field tackle on those guys cause all day they've been catching you in their rearview mirror."

The last call blessed both Ken and Bryce in a huge way.

Bill called and told of how much encouragement it was for him to hear of Ken, Bryce, and the other players on the Packers share that they have tough times and struggles also. At that time Bill was trying to sell his house and move his family out of a rough neighborhood.

"Listening to the show and listening to the big guys (Packer players) going through trials and errors too, you never think they have problems, but when they can admit them on the radio, it let's you know you're not alone."

He wasn't through blessing Bryce, Ken, and the Packers.

"A lot of times when I'm in the dumps I hear the guys testimonies, and it has really helped to bring our family back up, so I just want to thank everybody."

The fellas really appreciated the call. Paup added, "It's not easy while you're going through difficulty, but God can turn it around and use it to help others. I think that's part of the learning process to help other people and tell them God is sovereign and He'll see you through."

Before the end of the show, Paup and Ruettgers revealed that they pray for each other during the games.

We had to go. I closed with, "Bryce, don't think about us back home freezing while you're in Hawaii!"

My heart hurt every time I saw Paup in a Buffalo Bills uniform in 1995. I can't imagine how the Packers felt. As a fan, I felt bad, but not nearly as bad as the feeling of being cheated out of another opportunity to have him on the show.

Bryce Paup is the type of man who is quiet, but with the right crossing of his convictions, won't back down to anyone. Sometimes fans hope a player won't have his same success with their new team, after leaving via the free agency market. But not him. I know I'm not alone in wishing him nothing but the best. I miss him on the Packers, and I know thousands of Packer fans do too.

Just days after the '95 season ended, Lee Remmel told me something about Paup I found rather intriguing. He said, "Bryce Paup is going to be spending the off-season in Green Bay. He's looking for a duplex."

I thought, "A duplex? Why would a guy making that kind of money live in a duplex?" Well, maybe it's because he wants neighbors; or maybe just because he's a down-to-earth conservative Christian farm kid from Iowa, who has his feet planted firmly on the ground.

I was happy to know that at least in the summer months Bryce Paup's feet would be walking around Green Bay.

ADAM TIMMERMAN was a backup offensive lineman in 1995. When starter Aaron Taylor went down with a severe knee injury in the first round of the Playoffs, Timmerman stepped in and did the job the rest of the way.

10 - ADAM TIMMERMAN

We had just finished our maiden "Timeout" show in 1995. Because the Pack had a date with "Monday Night Football" the following week, it became necessary to tape next week's show.

Ken and I were making our way down the hall to the soda machine when we ran into a big, physically solid, red-head with a flat top haircut, wearing shorts, a T-shirt, and tennis shoes. I had only seen him up to this point as number 63 on the Packers.

Ken introduced me to him. "Adam, meet Steve Rose."

"Hey, how are things in Iowa?" I said. I knew it would help put the jittery man at ease.

It did.

Adam Timmerman is from Cherokee, Iowa, which is in the northwest part of the State. A laid back, farm community of 7,000, it's not in the middle of nowhere, but you can see it from there.

"Want something to drink?" Kenny asked him

"I'll have whatever you guys are having," he uttered politely.

"Steve, want to split one with me?" asked Ken.

"Sounds good."

Scotty, our faithful engineer, ushered the three of us into Studio B, of the WORQ. It was the production studio where we would record the show for playback next Monday night.

Adam seemed really nervous. Ken was his usual calm, cool, and collected self.

Scotty cued me after playing the intro to the program. "Welcome to another addition of the 'Timeout' program. I'm Steve Rose. Ken Ruettgers is here, and our special guest is Adam Timmerman. Don't call us tonight because this show is taped."

Ruettgers, who usually plays it pretty cool, decided to add some humor. "Yeah, I'm not here because I'm in Chicago."

"That's right. Ken's not here because he's not all there!" I countered, tongue in cheek.

I couldn't resist. Ken has yet to bonk me for picking on him. I wouldn't blame him if he did. He has taken some pretty vicious hits during the show over the years.

Timmerman, 24, and in his rookie season with the Packers told us about his days at South Dakota State and Cherokee, Iowa.

"Ken, you ever been in Iowa?" I inquired.

"I've flown over a few times, but I don't think I've ever driven through."

"You're missing out," said Timmerman.

When asked what it was like making the adjustment from a small town, the farm, and college life to the NFL, Adam said, "One day, I'm at a small college, working on a farm, and suddenly on not any NFL team, but the Packers!"

Farming is exactly what Timmerman might have been doing had he not made such an impression on the pro scouts while at tiny South Dakota State, an NCAA Division II school.

"The Miami Dolphins had called and said they were going to take me with their next pick," said the burly rookie.

The Packers beat the Dolphins to the draw. Timmerman was soon on a plane to training camp in Green Bay.

He gave thanks to his parents who brought him up in a church environment. "My Mom and Dad were great role models for me. They both work long work days and weeks. For me to put in 40-50 hours for the Packers is nothing compared to their schedules."

Timmerman was clearly in awe of his position as a Green Bay Packer. "It was during one of the TV timeouts during a pre-season game when it hit me what was going on. Brett was telling a cute story in the huddle, while I looked around Lambeau Field and said, 'Wow, I'm really here.' Even in the locker room I wanna run around and just start getting autographs," Timmerman candidly pointed out.

We talked a little bit about the difference between playing here rather than in New York or L.A.

"Ken, have you found it great to be in the small town?"

Without a hitch or hesitation he answered, "It's like Mayberry in the Andy Griffith Show. I go to the Shell station, and it's like, 'Hi Andy, Hi

Opie,'" he said with a southern drawl in his resonant voice.

"Ken and Adam, how important is it for you guys to actually be a little stocky, have a little spare tire to do your jobs well in the offensive line?"

Little did I know I had given Ruettgers an opening he had been looking for.

"Hey, it's not a spare tire," Ruettgers said with a smirk.

I caught where he was going immediately. "Here it comes. He's going to baffle us with some excuse.."

Ken finished, "It's not a spare tire, it's a 'Goal Line Muscle'."

"Didn't I tell you it was going to be some sort of creative smoke-screen?" I added.

Playfully as if to be offended, Ruettgers chided, "Hey, com'on," he smiled.

Adam was just sucking it up. He loved it.

Adam Timmerman married his wife Jana in 1993, while he was still in college and was quick to give her credit for her part in his arrival in the NFL. He thanked his new bride for reading him scripture at night at home and being 100% supportive.

Before we wrapped it up one detail was on Ruettgers mind.

Looking at Timmerman, Ken said, "I heard our wives are going shopping. Maybe there might be a change of plans," Ken said, insinuating he was a little concerned about the VISA taking a beating. He was kidding.

It was a wrap.

Ken had to leave and put the kids to bed. It was an unusually long night for the "Timeout" crew that night.

Afterwards, Adam and I chatted. We talked about Iowa and some other trivial stuff. I recall pleading with him to invest a good share of his money. I had heard so many of the horror stories of guys in pro sports "blowing it all." He assured me he was conservative and would take care of his finances.

Gazing at the wall, he said, "I always loved Mondays as a kid during football season cause it felt like a three day weekend with 'Monday Night Football'."

I stuck out my hand and replied, "Big man, next week you will be

'Monday Night Football'!"

I thanked him for coming in, and he said we had to get together sometime. Then we both split.

It was strange not to be in the studios doing the show live the next week. I was driving down Highway A, South of Neenah, capturing the beauty of the shore of Lake Winnebago, listening to the taped program. Ironically, I was going to Oshkosh to tape a TV program for Cablevision. It was fun hearing the taped interview because I knew when the funny stuff was going to come. I nearly drove off the road. Between Adam's innocence and Ruettgers's keen sense of humor, it was just neat to listen to.

As the ABC cameras panned the sidelines that night during the game, there was Adam Timmerman. I tried to imagine the thrill it must have been for the farm boy from Cherokee to be playing on "Monday Night Football." He was flashing that ever present grin, and somehow I knew he was experiencing something he could never put into words. One of those moments that is pure, perfect, and personal.

Adam Timmerman, a wonderful young man who will be heard from in the NFL for years to come, we hope, and so does the whole state of Iowa, especially those in Cherokee.

Timmerman went relatively unnoticed on the Packer roster, during his rookie year. He played primarily only on special teams until December 31, 1995, when Aaron Taylor went down with a serious knee injury against the Falcons in the playoff opener. Like a true pro, Adam stepped in admirably and made Packer fans proud. I'm sure there were some people in Cherokee, Iowa, who were feeling pretty good about him too.

11 - MARK INGRAM

rollicky, with a grin that would light up any room, Mark Ingram blessed the WORQ "Timeout" listeners during his 1995 appearance.

The night Mark was in was a bit hectic as the station was in the midst of their fall "Share-a-thon". As a listener supported, non-profit radio ministry, Q-90 takes a couple times a year to drum up financial support for broadcasting expenses. There couldn't have been a better witness of God's goodness than Mark Ingram that night to help in the cause.

Along with dozens of other people in the studios running pledges from the phone callers into the studio, we were a bit discombobulated with our seating assignments. Usually, I sat on the far left, on mike one. For some reason, Mark was there, and Kenny was in his usual chair in the middle, and I was sitting at mike C, the guest mike. Minor stuff, but I remember we had a little different atmosphere.

Nonetheless, Mark Ingram proved to be a very delightful, insightful man who shared right from the heart.

Being from Michigan, Ingram, who wore number 82 for the Packers in 1995, talked of being used to the cold when the issue of cold weather Green Bay football came up. He had played in New York for the Giants a few seasons before heading for the sun in Miami and the Dolphins. Before the 1995 season a trade with the Dolphins brought him to Green Bay. He came to the Packers at the time Ron Wolf was trying to convince Keith Jackson to come to Green Bay.

As a friend of Jackson's, Ingram said, "I've been on the phone a lot with him to try to get him to come here. I told him it was a great place to play." This date was Monday, September 25, and the Packers were just four games into the season. "I'm gonna send the Packers my phone bill."

I am sure they gladly paid it a few weeks later when Jackson caved in to the prodding from not only Ingram, but Reggie White, who had played with Jackson, under Buddy Ryan in Philadelphia.

Mark told of the many Christians on the Miami team that he was friends with, but said he was enjoying himself with the Packers.

Not only was I learning a lot with the radio crowd about Ingram, but admittedly Ken was too.

Mark and Ken jumped in with excitement when a new pledge came in for the "Share-a-thon". Mark got a real kick when I asked him to read the phone numbers.

Shockingly and without hesitation, he pointed out briefly that Dan Marino isn't shy about telling people how good he thinks he is.

As a rule a lot of these guys keep stuff like that to themselves. I appreciated it. Not from a stand point that we need to take glory in exposing or knocking people, but it's sometimes important speak out if there might be someone the kids are following who might not be healthy role model. We all need to be careful when we judge others. The Bible says, "He who is without sin cast the first stone." I live in a glass house myself and am the last guy who can throw stones, but I appreciated the honesty from Ingram regarding Marino.

As a Christian, Mark Ingram has been called with other disciples of Christ to be truthful and shine His light where there is darkness and to be the salt of the earth.

After the show as we walked up the steps to the first floor to go home, behind me about four stairs, I could hear Ken telling Ingram about when I asked Sterling Sharpe if he could handle a career ending injury, just weeks before it would happen. Ken teasingly was insinuating I might have put a whammy on the former Packer receiver. If I believed there was any truth to that statement, I would have taken him serious, but I know that God either initiates or allows things to happen to us. Sterling's deal had crossed the Lord's desk too, and in this life we just don't get enough answers sometimes.

"I'm glad he didn't ask me," said Ingram playfully serious.

I'm glad I didn't either.

Mark Ingram gave us all one more smile and a cordial handshake as he bid farewell. Nice man. Incredible smile. Any toothpaste company should be banging his door down.

12 - ANTHONY MORGAN

The parking lot at the studio was dim on Halloween Eve, the day after the Packers lost in Detroit, 24-16. The station is off Lombardi Avenue near Lambeau Field.

Ruettgers was hopping out of his vehicle as I was making my way across the blacktop which serves as fan parking during the season. He shook my hand as we met. Ken loves to shake hands. The size of his hands are awesome. My fingers were just reappearing as I gazed over at a silhouette coming towards us. Judging his size, I couldn't be sure that he was a player. As he came closer, the good looking shadow joined me and Ken.

"Steve, meet Anthony Morgan," said Ken.

"Hi, Anthony," I responded as our right hands clasped.

Morgan joined the Packers in the 1994 campaign. During the 1995 season he shared a lot of playing time and rotated starts with Mark Ingram.

It took about 25 seconds to realize what a privilege it was to meet a young man of the caliber of Anthony Morgan. Besides remembering that he played at one time for the Bears, I didn't know much about him. He'd only been number 81 to me.

At 6:00 p.m. sharp, the "Timeout" show sounded. We talked about the Lion loss, then Ken, as always, introduced our guest.

Now, I'll confess to you that I have heard many responses from a lot of athletes and sometimes we doubt their sincerity. For me, I get tired of hearing the cliches and pat answers.

Anthony shot from the hip, and when he talked about there being no "I" in team and the Packers being a "we" team not a "me" team, I believed him, and I think the listeners did too.

"Anthony, is it frustrating not having as many balls thrown to you as you'd like," I asked.

"Hey, if the route is one that doesn't call for me to catch a pass, it's my job to divert the defenders and take them to other areas on the field, and I'm happy to do that."

Again, you knew by the tone of his voice, over the air, and looking in his eyes in the studio, that he meant it.

Besides, being a good football player at Tennessee, where he was a three letter winner, he also excelled in track. "My mom was a track star, that's probably where I got my speed," he pointed out to the "Timeout" audience.

Ken mentioned that he had taken his kids trick-or-treating the day before, and he asked Anthony, "Did you trick or treat as a kid?"

"Yeah," he smiled with a childish grin. "It was fun back home in Cleveland."

I posed with Anthony for a picture, then he said his good-byes.

Without a doubt, and I say this in all fairness to all the guys on the Pack that Kenny has brought in to the show, Anthony Morgan had the greatest attitude. If you were looking for a guy who would go to war with you and throw himself cheerfully in front of enemy fire for you, take him. If you had 53 Anthony Morgans on any team, you couldn't lose. Even if you did, it would be done with such class you'd never tell the difference.

I hope along with many other Packer fans that Anthony Morgan is a Packer for a long time.

13 - DARIUS HOLLAND

One word comes to mind when you first look at Darius Holland: big! Even without his pads number 90 looked huge.

Ron and Karen Grosse, on the board of directors at the station, were standing out in the hall next to this large man. He had a two-tone navy blue letter jacket with rust colored leather sleeves. Three normal sized people could have fit in it.

Karen walked in to the studio where I was sitting, preparing for the show. "Who is that?" I whispered.

"I'm not sure," she said. "He talks so soft. I think he said Darius Holland, but I'm not sure."

I went out and shook his hand, started a conversation, and asked a few questions that might tip me off if it was him. Somehow, I was satisfied that it was. I think it was his Colorado Buffalo hat, I'm not sure.

Ruettgers brought his warm presence into the studio a minute later, and asked, "Hey Darius, what's up man?"

Gently and ever so politely, he shook Ken's hand.

Both big guys took off their jackets. Man, the size of their arms! I couldn't help but notice a huge, nasty scar on the left side of Darius Holland's left biceps. I was too chicken to ask what it was. I couldn't help but gaze at it throughout the night.

Kenny introduced Darius in the beginning of the show, and he was real bashful for the first bit.

It took a about fifteen minutes for me to realize and believe that a voice and spirit as meekly as Holland's could come from such a person of his size. The soft-spoken Holland, only 23 years old during this, his rookie season, goes about 6'3" and around 290.

By the time we got about thirty minutes into the show, Holland was at ease. It probably was the "mandatory ice cream" question that broke the ice cream, er, I mean ice. Each and every show, Kenny or myself pops this pressure packed question to each guest. "What's your favorite ice cream? How about blizzards from the Dairy Queen?"

"I like blizzards."

"What kind?"

"Butterfinger."

I perked up and said, "Me too!"

What a joy it was later to listen to this man give his testimony as to what the Lord has done in his life.

The former Colorado Buffalo credited Bill McCartney with much of his spiritual growth in the Lord. "Bill McCartney really helped me and many other people in Colorado."

Bill McCartney had, as head football coach at Colorado prior to Holland's graduating, accepted God's call to begin the "Promise Keepers", an organization dedicated to bringing out the best in Godly men.

We really didn't talk much about football throughout the show, but somehow it didn't matter. I did get a verbal shot from across the table to Darius about his furniture commercial that was running at the time. I took the time to tease Ken that if he had a full-time job, his sweet wife wouldn't have had to do commercials for Sentry grocery stores last year.

Afterwards, we took a picture that when I see it today just drops my jaws. I'm standing between Ruettgers and Holland. For some reason, Ken, on my left, looked like he had an extra biscuit for breakfast (maybe he stopped off for a Ben & Jerry's before the show), and Darius is on my right. I go about 5' 8" and 178, between trips to the refrigerator, and you can hardly see me in the picture. I look like a regularsize weiner in a giant, foot-long hotdog bun.

Later, when I saw the photo, it did dawn on me what Ron Grosse meant when he said jokingly while taking the picture, "Steve, stand up!"

Darius Holland. What a pleasant young man. The world can use a few more like him. Me, I'd like to have him for a bodyguard.

Nice guy, super nice kid.

14 - HARRY GALBREATH

I had heard a lot about Harry Galbreath before he was on the program during the 1994 season. After meeting and listening to him, I knew why.

My Dad was in the production studio watching and listening to the show. He had made the 90-mile trip up U.S. 41 from Eden, Wisconsin. It's one of those towns everybody claims to say they're from. Well, he and I are actually from there.

Early in the show, Galbreath told about his early days picking cotton down south to his football career with the Miami Dolphins. Very jolly and full of energy, the Packer right guard told of what it was like playing for Don Shula. "He would pick you out if you screwed up. Coach Holmgren is different. He won't single people out."

The audience had to be impressed with his candidness—call it being bold enough—to talk about Shula, a coaching legend, that honestly.

I was in great spirits, while Ken was his usual evenkeeled self. For some reason, Harry thought I was the funny guy. He laughed at all my little jokes, which is a sign of intelligence! As I picked on Ken going into the first break, Galbreath laughed, while looking at Ken, as if to say, "This guy is killing me," as the theme music came up.

I went to the other studio where my Dad was listening to the program. "Dad, come and meet Harry."

He followed me around the corner to studio A.

"Harry, meet my dad, David Rose."

"How's it going, big guy?" he asked standing and getting up politely.

"Great Harry, nice to meet you. Man, what a great game yesterday," he continued. (It was the Bear game at Lambeau that was a see-saw battle the Packers pulled out 35-28.) My Dad had ranted and raved about it to Ken, whom he had met just 20 minutes earlier.

We spent some time talking about the differences between playing in Miami, where he had been since 1988, and Green Bay. He signed as a free agent with the Packers before the 1993 season. The obvious difference is weather, but you really get the feeling not only from him, but others just how special a place that Green Bay is to play.

He credited his Grandma with bringing him up in the way of the Lord.

After the show, he and my dad really hit it off. My dad lucky to have survived putting up with me on our little dairy farm east of Eden, Wisconsin, sure enjoyed meeting Harry. I heard dad say, "If things don't work out with the team, I got a job on the farm for you."

They chatted enthusiastically until I said, "Let's get some pictures."

We got plenty. Some with Harry and Dad; Ken, Dad and Harry; Harry, Ken, and me, etc.

Harry had to leave. Then Dad, Ken, and I went and sat down, while Kenny signed some of his books for some of my friends. Dad had given Ken an official Rose-E-Vue family farm pen to sign the books with.

My Dad who has a crazier sense of humor than mine explained, "You can have that pen, Ken. It's got a solid gold clip. If you run into hard times, you can always melt it down."

Slouched forward signing a book, the cute remark went right over Ken's head.

The night Harry Galbreath was on the Q-90 FM "Timeout" program was one I'll always remember. So will my dad.

15 - KEITH JACKSON

All I'd heard about Keith Jackson is how much he hated the cold and how money-hungry he was. This was the picture that had been painted in front of me, and frankly, this was the opinion I had of him also. For me, this all vanished—in an hour.

Keith Jackson sat at microphone C next to Ken Ruettgers in the Q-90 studio for his appearance on the "Timeout" program. He had a white hat with a colorful insignia and a brown sweatshirt that covered a sharp white button-up shirt with no collar. It didn't take long to see he liked to have a lot of fun and laugh.

The intro played, which featured some jingle singers singing the "Timeout" jingle. Then the guy you hear on national spots with the deep voice said, "And now ... here are your "Timeout" hosts, Ken Ruettgers and Steve Rose." The music trailed as I introduced myself and Ken. Ruettgers wasted no time in introducing our guest. "Ladies and gentlemen, here's Keith Jackson."

Keith immediately started singing, "Timeout ... Timeout," just like the singers. "That's what we needed last night was a timeout," he said with his eyes rolling and a little grin on his face. The night before the Packers had lost in overtime to the Tampa Bay Buccaneers on ESPN.

"Keith, you must be a singer," I inquired.

"Only in the shower," he snapped. I knew from there he and I were going to get along just fine. Both nights Keith Jackson was on the show, it was just a gas!

Before Keith Jackson had arrived in Green Bay, there was some confusion as to his motives and his character as a football player. During the 1995 season, Jackson spent a good share of his time at home in Little Rock, Arkansas, while the Packers tried to lure him to Green Bay. Many folks thought he was greedy. Keith Jackson tells us his side of the story.

"Keith, what took so long for you to get to Green Bay," I asked.

"Well, I chose to not fight a war with the media because one thing they'll do is turn stuff around any way they want to."

"Isn't that the truth?" agreed Ruettgers.

Jackson was commenting about the rumors that had been floated by the media to the fans all over that Jackson was holding out for one reason: more money.

"So what happened?" I asked Packer number 88.

"At the end of the '94 season, I told Don Shula that I was going to retire. God had given me a vision to build a youth center in Little Rock called P.A.R.K., which is an acronym for Positive Atmosphere for Reaching Kids. In Little Rock,you don't know if your kids are going to live to see the next day or not. So I said 'If not me, who, if not now, when?" said Jackson.

Jackson continues to tell the story in a way we had never heard it before. "At the end of the season Don Shula came to me and said, 'I understand that you are going to retire.' I told him that was true. He said, 'Well, we're thinking of signing Eric Green.'" Green, a standout all-pro tight end was signed by Miami from the Steelers.

"That's true," Jackson told his former coach. "I assumed that it meant that I was free to leave the last year of my contract and just not play."

In the meantime, the Dolphins traded Jackson's right to the Packers. Fans in Green Bay were excited about the all-pro coming and helping the team. Fans didn't have all the details, according to Jackson.

"When the Packers called I told them I wanted to retire, that I had started the youth center. When the media heard that they thought it was about money. It wasn't me being selfish, I wanted to retire and help at the center."

As Jackson kept doing his part in Arkansas, Reggie White, who played with Jackson in Philadelphia, called. So did Mark Ingram who had played with Jackson in Miami.

Eventually Jackson was convinced by the players to come up and see what the Packers had to offer. He did, he helped, and the rest is history. So, had the media given the proper picture of Keith Jackson? I know my opinions were juxtaposed nearly 180 degrees as I listened to Jackson who has a very warm, sincere way of expressing himself.

Ken started teasing Jackson about the cold weather in Green Bay. Jackson makes no bones about the fact he is a "warm weather" guy.

"Keith and the receivers have to catch a ball and hold onto it. All I have to do is hold—a jersey," laughed Ruettgers.

Jackson made a comment that would make Lee Remmel, the great Packer public relations director and historian proud. "Did you know that the Packer-Raider game in 1993 was actually colder than the "Ice Bowl"? he pointed out. Where had he come up with that piece of trivia?

Ruettgers, who grew up in warm, sunny Southern California told his teammate, "The longer you're here, the more you get used to it. Now that I'm from Wisconsin, I'm an official—Cheesehead," acknowledged Ruettgers proudly.

"Keith, have you had the chance to get out of Green Bay?" I asked.

"I've been to Appleton, but not to Oshkosh. I gotta go down and get some of those clothes at Oshkosh B' Gosh. Send me some of those clothes," Keith joked.

Jackson hummed the "Jeopardy" theme as he pulled a name out of our rotating grocery bag full of names of entrants who wanted to win a copy of Ruettgers book.

Jackson talked about his faith for a bit and compared people like Ken to a famous Biblical man. "I always tell Ken that the offensive linemen are the "John The Baptists" of the football team. So much work to do in the trenches and not much glory," he pointed out.

I brought out the analogy of the hockey goalie being like an offensive lineman.

"Great analogy. What's that guy's name who's a goalie? Patrick Roy?" asked Ruettgers.

Weak, but up on my French, I said, "It's pronounced, Row-wah"

"Thanks for that pronunciation, that's a tough one, but what the heck, I'll just call him Roy," surrendered Ken. "I saw a special on him the other night. Being an offensive lineman is like that. You keep blocking and blocking and the goalies keeps saving and saving, but then a defensive lineman gets to the quarterback or the puck hits the net and a red light goes on, and thousands of people start screaming at you and calling you a sieve."

Keith Jackson laughed and empathized. He'd blown his share of plays throughout his career too.

Keith then sang a little gospel rap song that some of the players had come up with on the team bus, and Ruettgers backed him up. It was hilarious.

"Steve, these guys look at us like were crazy, but you know, they realize that you can be a Christian and still have fun!" he concluded.

After the show Jackson shared with me that Green Bay is the absolute perfect place to play professional football. It was much different playing in Philadelphia and Miami. We took some pictures of Keith, Ken, and me. Jackson held a Diet Coke can in front of him in mock endorsement.

"Coach Holmgren is great, the community is great, I love it here!" said Keith. Then he reached for his waist and grabbed his beeper. "Oh! It's my mama. When she calls, I gotta answer," he said as his voice trailed and he headed out of the station.

16 - KENT JOHNSTON
and STEVE NEWMAN

While watching the Packers on TV, it's tough to catch all of the men who are responsible for the Packers' success because of what they do behind the scenes. Two of these men come to the forefront of my mind. They are Kent Johnson and Steve Newman.

Kent Johnston is the strength and conditioning coach, while Steve Newman serves as team chaplain. These two unsung role models deserve a huge pat on the back for the part they play with the Packers. As leaders of the Green Bay "God Squad", these two men of great faith in the Lord are not seen on TV, but their presence sure is felt by the men on the team.

One prays and one prepares.

Steve Newman prays that God's will be done. Kent prepares the men physically for battle.

This book and tribute to the Packers wouldn't be complete without acknowledging the blessing I received from meeting them. Their level of integrity is above reproach.

I also appreciate all the other Packers who have chosen to let me into their lives, and I thank God for the opportunity to do the "Timeout" show. If you're ever breezing through Green Bay on a Monday night around six, tune it in. We'll be the ones talking about ice cream.

The Minister of Defense, REGGIE WHITE. No more need be said.

Nine

Reggie

eggie, this is God. Come to Green Bay!
Mike Holmgren, Packer head coach, had reached deep into his bag of tricks with that coy message he left on Reggie White's answering machine back in 1993. White was considering coming to Green Bay through free agency, but he made it clear he wanted to go where God wanted him. Today, he feels he made the right choice.

"I couldn't tell at first why God sent me here, but it didn't take long to see why. It's a great place to play football and the people here are great," said the ordained minister.

Just as the name Elvis is all that's necessary to introduce the late Elvis Presley, the name Reggie is all that's needed to bring attention to "the Minister of Defense". He *is* unarguably the leader, on the field and off, of the Green Bay Packers, and the most respected, outspoken Christian in all of sports.

What you see and hear is what you get with Reggie White. He speaks his mind. He's one of the very few bold enough to include a Bible passage (I Cor. 13) underneath his autograph. His personal priority scorecard tallies differently than the average person. His priorities, which are ordered by his faith in Jesus Christ, set him apart from many in the world.

"My family is important to me. Football is, too, but my Lord and my family come first." Reggie is also important to his team.

"If we had paid Reggie White $17 million and he had never played a down, it would have been worth it to have him on this team. Not only is he a force on the team, but in the community," says Bob Harlan.

The multi-talented, hard working man on a mission has a movie coming out called, *Reggie's Prayer*. Paul McKellips, a native of Neenah,

Wisconsin, directed the movie and is himself a die-hard Green Bay fan. "Obviously, I am a huge Packer fan," says Paul.

Reggie plays a retired football player who is inspired to reach out to teens. Sounds like it was an easy role for him to play. But this isn't just some "jockudrama" for White to use and capitalize on his fame.

"It appealed to me. I was excited when I read the script because Paul wrote it based on my character, my Christian lifestyle, and lots of principles that I believe in," said White.

White also has a book called, *In The Trenches*, due out in the fall of 1996. As always with White, the message is to share his source of strength, help, and hope with anyone who will listen, and even those who won't.

The fans nor the rest of the country didn't need any more new evidence that God pervades in Reggie's heart, life, and circumstances, but 1995 sure brought us more divine happenings. Reggie was one of a couple Packers of central focus. Along with Robert Brooks and Brett Favre, he was a real inspiration.

In 1995, it was an amazing hamstring injury healing that made believers out of many skeptics, while providing hope for others. This latest inexplicable "act of God" was barely a year after White claimed God had restored him physically from another injury. It was tendon damage in his elbow. He should have missed a couple weeks. He didn't. Let's take you back to November of 1994.

While co-hosting the "Timeout" Program, Ken Ruettgers, myself, and the Q-90 listeners learned the inside story about White's first medical miracle with the Packers. As Godincidence would have it, two days after Reggie White suffered the injury, our guest on the show was Packer head trainer Pepper Burruss.

That morning, Burruss gave some words of prophecy of a miracle that would be fulfilled within just a few hours at the Packer training facilities. Here's how it was revealed on the radio, two days before the Packer-Cowboy tussle on Thanksgiving Day:

"Pepper, give us an injury report for the Dallas game," I said. From what I'd heard, it sounded like there was no way White could play, but I was optimistic.

"Reggie, as everyone knows, hurt some ligaments in his elbow against the Bills Sunday," he said sadly.

Then he said these words that will live indelibly in my memory forever.

"Reggie will probably be out this week, but knowing his source of healing and strength, I wouldn't be surprised if he had a miraculous recovery and played."

Bingo, he called it!

Here's Pepper Burruss's account of "Miracle Number One" in November of 1994.

"Reggie was receiving massage, ice, and electrical treatment on his elbow. It was rare for a player to have been in the training room because usually the coaches require even the injured players to be at practice, even though they can't take part. In the training room, Reggie had this dejected look on his face and said, 'This could be one of those couple of weeks type of things couldn't it?' I said, 'Yes.'

Pepper left for practice as White fell asleep on the training room table listening to a "Take Six" tape. ("Take Six" is a Christian musical group.)

It happened again as Reggie was deep into a divine snooze. Through the authority and power of all the prayers for the wounded Packer hero, the healing work of the Holy Spirit went to work on White.

Pepper tells the rest of the story.

"I came up from practice, and he had this 'glow' on his face, and I looked at him and said, 'What? Tell me now you wanna play.'" Pepper was baffled and a bit skeptical.

"I can play," White said with hope abound on his face.

True to his word, he did play in the Dallas game. Burruss had fashioned a protective brace and had heavily taped the elbow. Even though the Packers lost the game, 42-31, God had shown himself true through his faithful warrior. In the Bible, God says that faith the size of a mustard seed can move mountains, and Reggie's faith and the prayers brought him through.

I will never forget the first time I met Reggie White. Kenny had introduced me to White at a Racial Reconciliation Rally which featured Reggie in Milwaukee. Two weeks later, he was a guest on the radio show. Like most weeks, Ken kept it to himself that White was going to be on in order to prevent any distraction at the studios.

Honestly, I don't recognize a lot of players when they come in. Like most fans, my view of the game and the Packer players is from the TV. With their helmets on, you can't see their faces. But that day, it was different. I usually stay pretty cool when the guys come in. I've learned that they are incredibly normal, friendly, and are uncomfortable when a fuss is made over them. My attempt to stay cool flew out the window as soon as I spotted White walk into the studio. My heart raced as I was in mid sentence with a question for Kenny at the time.

Reggie sat down. White's microphone wouldn't co-operate at first; it kept falling over. It was one of those goose-neck types that is adjustable, but the goose must not have felt too well that morning. Scotty, our engineer, fixed it.

Ken introduced the Packer defensive end and future Hall-of-Famer. I'm sure the audience was as peeled to his upcoming responses as I was.

For 6:30 in the morning, Reggie looked as fresh as a rose. His eyes sparkled. He was wearing a huge long black trench coat and a Packer baseball cap.

The first bit of business was the elbow miracle in November.

Ken asked, "Reggie, what's the most frustrating thing about skepticism of your healing?"

"It's that the media won't believe God healed me," he began.

I couldn't resist jumping in. "Reggie, I felt God telling you through the healing that he would not make a fool out of you for your faith."

He agreed. He further stated, "Had I called a press conference and said that I went to a witch doctor in Milwaukee or had some acupuncture, they would have understood and accepted that."

White was referring to the skepticism in the media. Even further, not all of the fans were convinced he was the benefactor of divine intervention. Always armed to give reason for the hope within him, White gave all credit and glory to the Lord for healing him.

"Reggie, why did you choose to come to Green Bay?" we asked.

"With each day it becomes more clear why we're here. We like it. The people here have been great. The fans here are the greatest. When I stepped on the field in 1993 for scrimmage and the place was full, I couldn't believe it." He finished, "To be honest, at first, I wasn't sure why God brought me here."

White's impact in Green Bay has gone well beyond just his teammates. Lee Remmel, the head of public relations told me, "I have to admit, I was a bit skeptical about White proclaiming, 'God called me to come to Green Bay.' Today I believe him. He backs up his words with his actions. He's a great man."

Former Packer voice Ray Scott said it so eloquently: "Reggie White is an outstanding person, who just happens to be a football player."

Also during the show with White, we talked about football, the racial issue, and Reggie's reason for living, working, and breathing, carrying the message of salvation through Christ.

The callers were just tickled to talk to their hero. A crowd was gathering in the hall of the radio station. They were getting a peek at their hero. They looked like cats in front of a fish store.

Reggie White, 295 pounds of love and class. A great football player, but an even greater man. A disciple on a mission to share his deep, abounding, and abundant faith with others.

The love affair between Reggie White, his family, and the community is such a great thing. The outburst of love shown to Reggie when the people of Wisconsin stepped in to help with money and prayers when his church in Tennessee burned touched White. Bob Harlan explains.

"Reggie told me, 'I can't believe how much these people love me here in Wisconsin,' after he was presented so much help for his church. I said, 'Reggie, you've given, and now it's their chance to give back.' They love and appreciate you."

Teri Barr grew up in Leopolis, Wisconsin, a little town an hour and a half northwest of Green Bay, and she says this team is very special with Reggie White, and the community is very fortunate.

"Reggie may not be the greatest football player ever, but he is the most incredible. His faith and motivation is a driving force on the team and for the fans."

Do you know of a person held in higher esteem, anywhere, in any profession, than Reggie White? How many people do you know that don't have an enemy in the world, like him? There has never been one negative thing written or said about him—ever—and we'd be surprised if anyone ever did.

KEN RUETTGERS has been a mainstay in the Packers offensive line for the past 11 years. As the 1996 training camp began, he was recovering from a recent knee surgery.

Ten

Oh, My Aching Comeback!

As they say, "One good miracle deserves another." Okay, maybe they *don't* say that; I made it up, but in this case it fits.

For my radio partner Ken Ruettgers, the 1995 season started out with a bang and lot's of pain. In the first pre-season game against the Saints, he suffered some injured ribs.

"Ken, did you fake an injury to put your name in the news to get some publicity for the book?" I joked. Ruettgers's book, *Homefield Advantage: A Dad's Guide to the Power of Role Modeling,* was ready to hit the bookstores. Of course, I was kidding.

The rib injury left him unable to play in the Packers second pre-season game in Pittsburgh. By next week, still with some soreness, Ruettgers was back in the lineup. Green Bay lost a close game to Indianapolis in Green Bay. The Colts won in overtime, 20-17.

Nine days later at about 5:40 p.m. Monday, August 28, I met Ken and his wife Sheryl in the parking lot of the WORQ studios for the six o'clock show. It was the first "Timeout" radio show of the year and began our second season together.

Ken was in a good share of pain as he shuffled gingerly across the hot asphalt of the radio station parking lot under the hot August sun. He'd gotten hurt again. Sheryl walked by his side. No matter how Ken Ruettgers feels or what's going on in his life, he is always loaded with encouragement. Despite his pain, he was no different.

"You look great, Bud!" he told me.

"Thanks, man," I responded thankfully as his huge hand swallowed mine. He winced as I shook it. I hugged Sheryl.

The huge offensive lineman was suffering from his latest injury. Just three days earlier, he found himself crumpled on the warm tundra of Lambeau Field, and I was there to see it. I hadn't been to a Packer game since that crazy "Snow Bowl" in 1985. My brother Gary was with me. Unlike the "Snow Bowl", it was a perfect evening for football. It was calm, sunny, and about 75 degrees at kickoff.

From above Lambeau Field in the club seats, I was downing cheese smothered nachos and slamming Diet Pepsi. It doesn't get any better than that, except maybe a Butterfinger Blizzard or pint of Ben & Jerry's Ice Cream.

It was in the second quarter when the Pack was about to score. They ran a running play to the right in the end zone right in front of us. As they unpiled, I watched Kenny get up. He reached his right hand to his lower back and stretched slightly back. He looked to be in extreme discomfort.

In a split second, as if dropped by the blast of a deer rifle, he dropped to his knees, then to all fours near the goal line.

A hush enveloped the stadium.

I thought, There's my radio partner and friend lying there in pain, helpless in front of 60,000 people. Is he gonna be okay? Very selfishly, I pondered, Will he be all right to do the first show of the season with me on Monday?

Very selfish, but honest.

I also remember thinking, Oh, my God! What's Sheryl feel like, seeing her husband lying there? What goes through a wife's mind when she sees her wounded warrior motionless on the battlefield? Does she picture him helpless in a hospital wondering if he'll walk again?

In my insensitivity, I was hoping he would not only return to help the Packers win but be able to do a radio show. God forgive me.

Pepper Burruss and the Packer medical staff quickly came to his aid.

After a few minutes Ruettgers was pulled to his feet and escorted to the sidelines as the capacity crowd prayerfully applauded in hopes that he would be okay.

Ken didn't see any more action that night, and preliminarily it appeared a good share of his season was probably in jeopardy too.

Three days later Ken, Sheryl, and I were walking slowly down the steps to the radio studio. Ken was lucky to be walking—anywhere. I had my hand gently on Ken's lower back to support him as we went downstairs to the studios.

"How's it feel, big man?" I asked.

"Sore."

"What happened?"

"I got kicked in the back."

"What did it feel like?"

"I thought my back shattered."

Then I thought, What must it feel like to be laying there with a stadium full of people gaping at you, while you're wondering if you'll ever walk again?

By eerie coincidence, there happened to be a vertebrae chart on the wall at the bottom of the steps. The radio station, ironically, is in Dr. Ray Roddin's Pro Care Chiropractic Building. Ken pointed to the exhibit as he explained to me what had happened with four tiny bones in his back.

"These are the two little deals, just off on my backbone that are cracked."

It wasn't a real professional diagnosis, but even I, the highly uneducated ex-farm boy, could follow that. What he was telling me was that basically he was walking around with a broken back!

Later, Ken learned he had not actually been kicked in the back like he originally thought. Here's what actually occurred.

Standing upright making a block, his backbone got pinched and contorted in such a way that the muscle inside the backbone let out a tremendous charge. Kind of like the recoiling of a rubber band. Like a bolt of lightning, it gave the same sensation, although different, as if he'd been kicked in the back.

I could relate a bit. I remembered a basketball injury that felt similar, only it was the back of my leg. I remember backpeddling and turning around to see who kicked me in the back of the calf. When I saw no one there, I got scared. It's like a shock with someone kicking you. I don't know what's worse the pain or the frightening nature of it.

We made our way to the studio. After a short prep time, we hit the air waves at our new time, Mondays from 6:00 to 7:00 p.m. Last year we were on Tuesday mornings from 7:00-8:00 a.m; quite a change.

I noticed there were a lot less cobwebs in the brain for both of us. The listeners seemed to like the new time.

Charles Jordan was supposed to be our guest, but he showed up for Mike Holmgren's show or something. Can you imagine how he felt when he realized he could have been on "Timeout" instead of only Holmgren's show on TV? No, we don't have any of those perks like watches or gift certificates the other shows use to lure people there; we don't have to. Seriously, a lot of the guys have said they appreciate the "loosy-goosy", laid-back nature of the show with me and Ken. We just sit back, talk about football, and ice cream!

Without Jordan, Sheryl Ruettgers sat in as our guest. We never missed a beat. No one knew the difference. I enticed her to tell us something about Ken that might make him blush; something that even the radio listeners might be able to tell he was embarrassed by! I asked Sheryl playfully, "So does Ken have pajamas with footballs on them or anything?"

"No," she laughed.

Maybe the closest we came to making "the big fella" edgy was when Sheryl said years back Ken would sit around the pool during his holdouts at their home in Bakersfield, California. (Ruettgers has gone through three contract negotiation holdouts during his 11-year career with the Packers.)

"Do you think you can play next week against the Rams?" I inquired of Ken.

"I'll try to see if I can put my shoes on by myself before trying to play. Right now I can't even do that," he acknowledged painfully.

At home against the Rams, without Ruettgers' services, the Packer offensive line had a whale of a time trying to protect Brett Favre. It was no surprise that the pressure was coming heavy from the right side of the Ram defensive line, the left side lacking Ken's presence in the offensive line. This was from the zone Kenny would normally be protecting.

On Green Bay television sports, they showed Ken with his servant's heart delivering water, towels, and encouragement to his teammates during the game. Wearing a white Packer polo shirt that was big enough to show a movie on, the local TV cameras panned the veteran bringing towels and water to his teammates. Ken watched helplessly as his team fell short, 17-14, to the St. Louis Rams. It would be the only home game the Packers would lose in 1995.

It didn't take a rocket scientist to surmise that had the Packers have had Ruettgers anchoring down the fort at left tackle, the Packers might have won the game. Nothing against Joe Sims; he's just not Ken Ruettgers. They certainly would have been more competitive with Ken in there.

"I have never been hit so many times in my life," said a beat-up, exhausted Brett Favre after the contest.

"Don't comment on this, but a lot lesser of a man might walk into Ron Wolf's office and ask to renegotiate his deal," I joked with Ken before the show the next night.

He just smiled and took a swig from his Dr. Pepper. He didn't have to say anything. Ken Ruettgers is a winner. Winners don't partake in gossip or provide sparks that turn into flames that build the fires of controversy. It's not him. I just wanted to playfully make a point, and I did.

Charles Jordan did make it in for the show the next time, and it went well. An infamous, memorable moment was caught on tape during this show, and it will remain recorded in my mind also.

After a brief light discussion about the loss, we opened up the phone lines for calls for Ken and Charles. A gentlemen had sadness in his voice and asked the sore tackle, "Ken, have you ruled yourself out for next week?"

The Packers had a grudge match on tap with the Chicago Bears on "ABC's Monday Night Football" the next week. With positive hopes but a shade of disappointment, Ruettgers replied, "I never count out the miracles of the Lord. A lot of people are praying for me."

Then he made this classic statement I will never forget.

He dipped his face slighted toward me, peered into my face with a twinge of dejection, but also a glimmer of hope, and said, "I don't know if this back thing is high on God's priority list, but I've been praying a lot, and biblically it says if a son asks his father for a plate of bread, he's not gonna put snakes on it. I hope His answer is yes … not wait."

During the week, Ken was still awfully sore and getting a lot of treatment. The Packers listed him as day to day for the coming Monday. As the game inched closer, the sports was still full of coverage speculating Ken's return. Hopeful wishes were put to questions as to whether Ken felt ready.

"Will you be ready to play on Monday night in Chicago?" asked a local TV reporter for an affirmative answer from the wounded giant.

As he had so delicately done with this question earlier on his radio show, he jokingly replied, "I'll see if I can put my shoes on first." Then turning serious, he said, "If we had to play today I couldn't, but we still have a couple days and I haven't ruled out a miracle."

"So you're not ruling out playing," they questioned.

"No, I haven't ruled out a miracle."

You see, miracles happen. Ken had watched one with his teammate Reggie White in 1994. White rebounded from the injured list to play in the Thanksgiving game in Dallas.

So the Packer fans prayed that Ruettgers could return to help their beloved team. The Monday night ABC nationally televised game's audience was the first to find out God's answer to all of the prayers. It was a resounding—yes!

Along with Ken's amazing appearance in the Bear game in the national spotlight, he played well and they showed him on TV a lot. Ken's misfortune, through his injury and recovery, was very timely as fellow Bakersfield native Frank Gifford put in a plug for Ken's book during the ABC national telecast.

So, in just days, Ruettgers went from extreme personal discomfort to back into the bone-crushing, constant, human bodily sacrifice of professional football. You know, it's not like he's a dance instructor; we're talking collisions! Yes, repeated, violent, physical trauma that would knock the common man senseless.

Ken Ruettgers has told me more than once that "football is the closest thing to peace-time war there is. That sounds kinda like an oxymoron, but it is true." I believe it.

Ken said later he'd played in the Bear game nearly pain-free, with no medical injections whatsoever! It *was* indeed a miracle. Just a couple weeks later, Pepper Burruss was our guest and confirmed this fact. He gave us the real nuts and bolts of just how the odds were stacked against Ruettgers because of the nature and severity of his injury.

"When Ken's back injury first was reported, it was thought that he only had two little bones broken in his back. Well, actually there were four. Ken didn't feel it was necessary to tell anyone that the injury was worse than everyone thought."

Burruss continued to back up his case that Ken's recovery was mystifying to say the least. "Ironically, just a few days ago, in a respected sports medical journal, they did a report on the seriousness of the injury. Approximately 30 players with the same type of fracture took an average of 31 days to return to playing. That was with one to two bones broken," commented the Packer head trainer.

Ken had four bones broken, and his recovery had taken only half the usual time to recover!

"All the credit goes to the Lord, not the trainers, for Ken's ability to play that quickly because Kenny was on the long end as far as the severity of the back injury and the short end as far as recovery," admitted Pepper.

Another Packer miracle? It sure looks like it.

Ruettgers was a little frustrated with the media's response to his healing. "I talked to the reporters and gave all glory to God. I say that not to build up myself, but to steal a line from Reggie, if I'd said, 'I went and had some acupuncture or saw a hypnotist, it would have been big news. As much as this country's people are praying and see prayers being answered, I wonder why people are so skeptical? It blows me away."

I had told Ken just a few days earlier in a phone call, "Ken, I truly believe in my heart that God used your rib and back injuries to bring your name into the press to help promote your book. Now with the back thing, look what's happening?" I observed.

After the Monday night game, the Friday before the Giants game, Ken confirmed my suspicions about what God may have been up to in Ken's life. One the phone, Ken said, "Steve, I think you might be right about God using my injuries to bring an awareness to help the book."

I knew it; God had used Ken's pain for His gain.

Ken Ruettgers, Reggie White, and a good many other Green Bay Packers love God and are trying in the best way they know how to touch others by sharing this message with others. When they aren't using words, they are showing it on the field.

The message is that a life reconciled to God is a life that will be of joy, peace, beauty, and unfolding of purpose in that life. They aren't ashamed to share their experiences and vulnerabilities, including weaknesses to make the point and helping others.

If we in need of a miracle, God says bring your hopes to the cross. The pool of living water there runs deep, and it's only a leap of faith away.

Eleven

A White Night

I walked into the kitchen, set my briefcase on the counter, and pressed the play button on my answering machine.

"Steve, Ken Ruettgers calling. Just wanted to let you know I tried to stop by the radio station this morning and the doors were locked. I know you guys are trying to keep out the riffraff, and you were successful. I didn't make it in. I got some folks workin' on a couple deals for us —and want you to know we're still on for Tuesday, so keep that in mind. I'll stop in and see you Monday morning. Bye."

Boy, was I glad to know we were still on for Tuesday. What was going to happen on Tuesday, November 8, 1994? Ken Ruettgers had asked me to join him and Steve Newman, the Packer chaplain, on a trip him to Milwaukee for Reggie's Racial Reconciliation Rally.

On the morning of the rally during the radio show, Ken told how a major part of Reggie White's ministry is laden with a passion for the human race to get together, forgive, forget, and bury the hatchet. It's a tall order, but as a tremendous role model in the community for his family, the team, friends, and most of all, for Christ, White's constantly working hard to achieve that.

Ken added, "Let's not just condemn people for being prejudiced, but let's do something about. Let's break down the barriers and bridge the gap. Let's get the church involved. We want to go down and let iron sharpen iron, hold each other accountable.

"Be sure to come to Milwaukee to the rally tonight. Bryce Paup, Mark Brunell, Guy McIntyre, and myself with be there to support Reggie and I hope you will too," said Ken as we wrapped up the program.

About one o'clock, Ken followed me to Neenah. We stopped at Mc-

Donald's where my wife Kim works. You should have seen the looks as Ken walked in. Many were in awe, especially Lou, the store manager. As he shook Ken's hand, he had this look on his face like, "Man, is he big!"

We walked to the back of the store where Ken met Kim. Kelly, an employee sitting with her, spotted Ken. She uttered, "Kim, they're here!" Forewarned, they were waiting with great anticipation for the extra large customer to come in and have a couple of Big Macs. Lou bought lunch. Ken signed the sweatshirt Kelly was wearing—between bites of his Big Macs.

"Thanks," she said with the enthusiasm of a seventh-grader. She was in her 20s.

"My pleasure ... thank you," Ken replied.

We wolfed down the complimentary burgers, said our goodbyes, and left to go to my place so I could change from my St. Vinny De Paul pants to a suit and tie.

Mike Rougeoux, a friend of our family, stood in shock when Ken stepped out to greet him on the sidewalk in front of our house. "Guess I have something to talk about at work today!" he said.

We were on the way to Milwaukee by three. Kenny worked a lap-top computer as Steve Newman guided Ruettgers's white Suburban down U.S. Highway 41. Ken was recording a couple of the "Role Model Minute" scripts directly onto computer disc.

"How does this sound?"

Ken played a message back, his voice with music behind it.

"Hi, this is Ken Ruettgers of the Green Bay Packers. Besides love, the greatest gift that God has given to man is the ability to make choices. This gift literally gives us a choice of where we want to spend eternity."

It sounded great!

We reached the outskirts of Milwaukee by 4:30, an hour and a half after we ate at Macs. I was amazed when Ken said, "Let's get something to eat."

"We just ate," I said. "Are you hungry again?"

Steve Newman just smiled.

The big offensive lineman smiled at me. "I have to keep my goal line muscle around my waist in good form."

Sounded like a good excuse to me.

Shortly after, we found ourselves at a downtown Cousin's Sub shop, close to the Milwaukee Auditorium where the Racial Reconciliation Rally with Reggie White was to be held. Later, we returned to Ken's vehicle. Although being a self-admitted jeans and tennis shoes sort of guy, Ken Ruettgers did look a little uncomfortable that day. Try to picture the Incredible Hulk dressed in a navy blue sports coat, white open neck shirt, gray slacks, and black penny loafers. He had yet to put on his tie. There was no sense putting it on any sooner than he had to. Tonight for his friend Reggie he'd sacrifice.

The trip to the Milwaukee Auditorium took only minutes. Around six o'clock, we were "waved in" the back door. It was an incredible feeling. Two minutes later we were VIP'd into a room with a huge group of promoters, organizers, musical guests, and Reggie White. I couldn't help but think to myself, "Why am I here?" It was like walking in a dream. Then I experienced a huge thrill as Ken led me to the main man.

"Reggie, this is Steve Rose. He does the radio show with me."

White nodded very graciously, shook my hand, and made me feel like I was the most important person in the world. "Good to see you. Thanks for coming."

"Thank you, Reggie."

I was impressed. There he was, the guy we have all heard so much about. I always wondered if he was for real. He is! In those 10 seconds, I got a crash course in understanding why God has raised this man up in his kingdom. Reggie cares. He passionately serves people. Many will say it, but here he was 120 miles down the road from home, showing it, especially on his day off.

Like a little child who'd just met Santa Claus, I watched White sit back down and sign some footballs. They were auctioned off for $500, each—a bargain.

Steve Newman came over to White. "Reggie, you need some prayer?" They prayed.

I walked over and met B.J. Weber from the New York Fellowship. He is the director of the International Fellowship Outreach Ministry. They sponsored the event.

I looked to the other side of the room. Some other players had just arrived in the same spirit as Ken to support Reggie.

First, Ken introduced me to Guy McIntyre. He'd played all those years for the World Champion San Francisco 49ers. Three Super Bowl rings. He was wearing one of them. Wow!

Then Mark Brunell stepped forward at Ken's request to say "hi" to me. Not far removed from playing quarterback in the Rose Bowl, Mark was then playing backup to Ty Detmer and Favre.

Bryce Paup meekly extended his hand my way. The underrated Packer linebacker was very kind.

As I observed how friendly and sensitive Paup appeared to be, I couldn't help but think how bad Paup must have felt when Randall Cunningham hurt his knee. Bryce sacked him in 1991 during the season opener. The Packers lost, 20-3, but the Eagles lost Cunningham for the season.

Then I experienced another treat. I met Sara White, Reggie's better half, as well as their children. Cute kids. A wonderful blend of both their parents. I couldn't help but wonder what life must be like for them with a famous Dad. Do they get bothered beyond comprehension in school? Are the expectations of those precious children way too high? What's it like to be them?

Mark Brunell stood to my left. Bryce Paup was in a soft chair four feet across from me. Ken towered next to him. Guy McIntyre was sitting on a plush couch to Ken's left.

Out of the left corner of my eye I saw a Domino's Pizza kid with a pile of pizzas.

Within moments, we were munching on the pizza. I couldn't believe I was eating again. Ken was "pigging out" too. This was two meals in an hour, three in about four hours! I didn't even bother to tease him. He would have just talked about filling out his "goal line muscle" some more.

As we broke bread, I heard some of the cutest dialogue, between some of the coolest guys, I've ever heard.

To my left I heard Mark Brunell teasing Bryce Paup. "How's it going Bryce 'Snap-Crackle' Paup?" Chris Berman, the sports nickname king, had placed Paup in his identity trophy case on ESPN sports television, and Brunnel couldn't help but rub it in a little.

Paup just grinned and shrugged his shoulders.

Four feet in front of me, Guy McIntyre teased Ruettgers. "How's the president of the Rush Limbaugh Fan Club tonight?" Guy followed his comment with a deep, hearty laugh.

Ken teasingly retorted something about the former San Francisco 49er being a little too liberal.

"I'm not liberal, just a compassionate person," laughed McIntyre. Then the glib lineman with three Super Bowl rings proceeded to drop his piece of pizza on the floor—cheese first. He picked it up and ate it. It reminded me of something I'd do. A few carpet fibers aren't going to hurt you. It makes good floss for the teeth, although I do worry about getting a hair ball now and then.

I also talked to Mark Brunell about his college football days in Washington.

Bryce Paup and I talked about Iowa. He grew up in Scranton. I spent a couple years in my early radio days in Clarion. We chatted about farming. After 10 minutes of conversation, I found it very hard to believe that this mild-mannered man could turn into such a mean quarterback terror on Sundays.

I moved over to Guy McIntyre. "What's that goofy thing you wear on the back of your neck during the games?"

"It's a modern day neck roll. You remember those things we used to wear around our necks that looked like life preservers? This looks different, but protects my neck. I hurt it one time years ago, and I just got used to wearing it. Now everybody kind of recognizes me by it."

I asked, "What's Joe Montana like?" McIntyre had played on the 49ers for many years with Montana.

With our stomachs full, we gathered in a circle for prayer for the evening's events. I recall clenching Bryce Paup's hand as Reggie asked in prayer that God's will be done.

Before heading out onto the floor, Reggie asked his teammates, "Any of you guys want to say something tonight?" They all pointed at one another like a bunch of seventh graders.

The consensus among players was that Ken, being the elder statesman, should address the crowd. They gang-tackled him big time. With a smile Ruettgers agreed to speak.

Then marveling at White's attire, Ken grabbed the lapel of Reggie's coat, gazed at the whole suit, and remarked, "I gotta get me one of these." Everybody laughed.

Ken will probably rush out and get one the day he starts enjoying losing, signs with the Chicago Bears, or quits eating Ben & Jerry's ice cream. It ain't gonna happen.

At around ten to eight, the mood turned from laughter to business as Reggie led us out to a thunderous, warm applause from about 4,000 people.

We were seated in the front row. Steve Newman was on the far left next to Guy McIntyre, who sat by Paup, then Brunell. I sat next to Ken. Wisconsin State Representative Bob Welch sat to my right. Reggie was on the other side of the aisle.

I read through the bright orange program headlined, *An Evening Of Reconciliation,* to follow the order of the events.

Before we got deep into the program, an usher suggested I sit in the second row. I agreed. I felt kind of awkward sitting in the row with the players anyway. I got up and moved. Ken turned to say something to me, but I was gone. Then he looked around and spotted me. "What are you doing? Get up here!" he bellowed.

"The guy said I should—"

"Big deal! Get up here!"

I didn't argue.

That made me feel good. It was as if Ken had said, "You are an important person and my friend."

As the festivities progressed, I thought, This is really something for me a highly uneducated ex-farm boy whom the Lord rescued from the pits of alcoholism just a few years earlier. How is it I am here sitting with these guys?

B.J. Weber gave an opening greeting to the crowd before the choir sang. Then Ken was introduced.

From deep in his heart, he shared one of his favorite Bible verses. "Christ said we are to 'love the Lord thy God with all your heart, mind, and soul.'" I was proud of him.

To a warm applause Reggie White then took the center stage. He spoke from his heart about the need for the races to get together and mend their differences.

Personally, I felt the conviction. No pun intended, but there is an element of irony when you think of someone by the name of White helping address the black and white issue. He was right, however; it was time to do make amends, to do something about our past thoughts and actions. We should all wrench our prejudices from our souls, bury them forever in the bowels of Hell where they belong, and replace them with the brotherly love of Jesus.

Reggie White is a very humble man who knows his place. However, he did want to make his position in Wisconsin clear to the large contingent that night.

White said, "I hear you have a 'Big Dog' here in Milwaukee.". He was referring to Glenn Robinson who was taken with the first pick in the 1994 NBA Draft. White who arrived in Packerland in 1993 continued, "Before the 'Big Dog' was, the 'Big Dog' is!" The crowd erupted in a loud roar of approval. He had made his point quite respectfully and eloquently. Everyone agreed. I'm sure Glenn Robinson did too.

White spoke with the fortitude of an old-time preacher and the heart of a lion as he bared his soul, telling of the hurt that invades his heart because of racism. He spoke about it for nearly 45 minutes.

"One of the things that disturbs me is the racism within the Church. There is still prejudices—even in the Church. People need to get off this rift of color and denomination. God has given us all a job to do, and while we're arguing over things that don't matter, a lot of people are dying spiritually for no reason."

White also challenged the people to try some different measures in dealing with some of their trials, troubles, and burdens. "If you're struggling with drugs, try Jesus! If you're looking to fill that void inside you, try Jesus! If you can't forgive your fellow man on your own, try Jesus. He'll help you," cried the Packer spiritual leader.

As Reggie's message neared it's end, it became time to put egos, philosophies, and prejudices aside and take them to the foot of the cross. It was time to do some heavy duty reconciling.

Reggie challenged, "Right now I want the blacks, whites, and any other races here to get up out of your seats and go apologize to one another. Go find someone from another race and ask for forgiveness. Right now!"

No one in the place hesitated. Who isn't going to listen to Reggie White? I believe God, through the Holy Spirit, was speaking through Reggie's lips.

Looking like Danny DeVito and Arnold Schwarzenegger, Ken and I hopped up onto the huge stage and greeted the black choir with hugs and handshakes. I embraced at least 20 to 30 people.

"Will you forgive me?" I asked a lady in her thirties.

"Yes," she said as her voiced cracked.

If you've never tried this humbling apology thing, you have to do it at least once. The confession, repentance, and apology had helped to lighten my spirit.

The Lord was healing thousands of hearts throughout the Milwaukee Auditorium. It quickly took on an atmosphere of peace and forgiveness. The wall of prejudice was penetrated and knocked down.

I looked around. There were tears everywhere. It was time to check your pulse if this didn't move you.

Before I sat down, a tall guy from New York whom I'd met earlier told me he was sorry for the sins of his race against mine. "I'm sorry too, brother," I said.

Minutes later, White invited people to take the greatest leap of faith yet. The ordained Baptist minister and Packer lineman offered the opportunity for anyone to come forward and accept Jesus Christ as their Lord and Savior.

In the Bible God promises that all who make this commitment can know they will go to heaven when they die and live with Him in heaven forever. As a bonus, Reggie explained that the Holy Spirit would come into the hearts of those making this commitment tonight and begin directing their lives.

White's words are backed up with a written guarantee in John 6: 47, where it states: "Verily, verily, I say unto you, he that believeth in Me hath everlasting life."

It was an offer many didn't refuse that night. There were street people as well as astute business people who could avoid the truth no longer. The truth that until we recognize that we need Christ as Savior, we're lost.

Ken and the Packer players were mobbed by autograph seekers. Just a minute earlier, I had been standing right next to my friend. Within a short time we became parted by a wave of crushing fans.

A minute later Ruettgers looked around and asked, "Where's Steve Rose?"

"I'm over here!" I yelled.

"Let's go man!"

We tried to force our way to the back door where we had come in. Reggie White helped to scatter the faithful by announcing the players had to get home and rest so they could make practice by 7:45 the next morning. Green Bay was still two hours and 120 miles north.

We met Steve Newman where we had been earlier backstage.

"Reggie, can you sign an autograph for Kim?"

"Sure."

I didn't have any paper on me. I pulled a First Assembly church bulletin out of my suit jacket. We found a pen. With nothing to write on, Reggie's signature was barely readable and you had to really use your imagination to make out his trademark, "I Cor. 13," To Kim. Whether you could read it or not really wasn't important.

"Sara, please?" I asked Mrs. White.

She wrote, "Kim, sure wish you could have been here with us tonight, Sara White."

Not only do I wish Kim could have been with me that night, but all of you as well.

The chatter became silence as Ken, Steve, and I left the building through a side door.

I still see in my memory the silhouettes of Guy McIntyre and Ken Ruettgers in the Milwaukee night, having a "heart-to-heart." It was none of my business what they spoke about, but there may have been some more forgiveness going on between the races by the two great friends. They shook hands, and Ken met Steve and me in the car.

Shortly, we hit highway 41 and pointed for home. Just outside of the city we stopped for gas, candy bars, and soda, then were off. Ken, who hadn't driven on the way down, was behind the wheel. Steve Newman was in the front seat and I had the whole back seat to myself. Propped in the middle to see each of them, I got the guts to ask a question I always wanted to bring to Ken.

"What kind of a guy was Tony Mandarich?"

Tony was the "Incredible Bulk" who came out of Michigan State in 1989. *Sports Illustrated* had made him out to be the next Superman. With high hopes, the Packers drafted him ahead of Barry Sanders, who turned out to be a star running back for the Detroit Lions. He still is going strong today.

Ken pointed out, "During his second year, I got together with Tony to show him some of my old game films from when I struggled during my career. I wanted to give him some comfort, to show him that I, too, struggled early in my career."

I further probed, "Do you think the *Sports Illustrated* thing made it almost impossible for him to live up to the expectations?'

"Yeah, it's tough. The job of the media is to build you up beyond belief, and it can make it very tough."

Ken Ruettgers knows first hand. He was a first round pick of the Packers in 1985, the seventh overall pick in the whole draft.

Mandarich was released by the Packers, and after being out of football for a few years, he was signed by the Indianapolis Colts for the 1996 season.

It was about 10:00 p.m. as we breezed past Fond du Lac about 60 miles north of Milwaukee. I thought about a turtle sundae from Gilles Frozen Custard, a Fond du Lac favorite.

Ken reached for his cellular phone and called his wife to tell her he'd be back home in an hour. "You guys need to make a call?"

"Nope," the chaplain and I echoed in stereo. We both agreed our wives probably wouldn't be losing any sleep over us and passed.

We, and our conversation, had started to run out of gas.

Then, in the blinking of an eye, we exited on Breezewood Lane in Neenah. In minutes, we pulled into my driveway.

"Thanks, Ken." I said.

"Thanks for comin' man."

"See you, bro," echoed Chaplain Steve Newman.

By midnight I was in bed reflecting on what had happened that night. I wouldn't have believed it if I hadn't have been there myself.

The lesson and moral of the story for the evening? Even with the Packers, there are some things bigger than football. The bold performance the "Big Dog" gave before that crowd was heart warming and challenging. I felt conviction to be more bold in sharing my faith and to look for more opportunities to reach out and help others. I had needed to take another leap of faith, and believe that I too should walk forth in my ministry.

The glimpse of the vulnerabilities of the Packers I met left me with an incredible new respect for them. It will live on with me much more than any memories of things they have done and will ever do on the football field.

As I lay in the darkness, I thought, Is it co-incidence or God-incidence that all those guys profess a love for and have a personal relationship with Jesus Christ?

More than great football players, my friends in Sunday green and gold had given me a glimpse of the Savior. In Reggie White, I had not only heard a sermon, but I had seen one and made a friend as well.

When you get right down to it, these guys, as well as many like them around the NFL, are big-hearted folks with a love for people. The players won't always let you see it underneath their helmets; they are precious in their spirits.

Since that night, November 8, 1994, I believe this love is still being shared in monumental proportions with the fans and people of Wisconsin and the entire country.

By 1995, Robert Brooks, Anthony Morgan, and others shared pure love and appreciation with the people in the front rows of the end zones in Lambeau Field. God's love. The kind that provides the energy for the shoes making those leaps of faith.

There are not only angels over Green Bay, but some in the huddle. The same ones I saw in Milwaukee that night.

HARRY GALBREATH gave good service to the Packers during his short stay in Green Bay.

Twelve

Packer Passion:
Here, There, Everywhere

We're a little bit like the Green Bay Packers. The entire state of Kentucky follows our basketball team." Those words came out of the mouth of Rick Pitino, the University of Kentucky basketball coach minutes after his team won the National College Athletic Association (NCAA) championship in 1996.

If you're under the impression this "Packer thing" is contained to just Wisconsin, think again. This allegiance, unique to any sport, clearly holds no boundaries. It reigns supreme at the Watering Hole in Reno, Nevada, and Gabe's By The Park in Packer unfriendly Minneapolis-St. Paul, Minnesota. Packer fans are everywhere. For good measure, throw in the folks at the Horse Creek Station in Hoback Junction, Wyoming, too.

America's Pack, the official fan club of the Packers, boasts thousands of members from all 50 states and 13 foreign countries. *Packer Report*, which they publish, reaches thousands of Packer fans all over the world. Todd Korth, from *Packer Report* says, "The history of the team, combined with the loyal fan support, make the Packers special. Win or lose, the fans are there. I don't think you can say that for all the other teams."

The Packers and their loyal following is hardly a secret anywhere. The stories of incredible Packer fans loaded with undying dedication to the green-and-gold are many, but we have found just a few special Packer fans from outside the Dairy State that canvass the United States of America.

Granted, it is normal for one of the thousands of Packer fans from a-round the country to come here and see a game. But James, Ruth, and Patrick Breeden aren't normal in that respect and neither are their num-erous trips each season all the way from Mount Washington, Kentucky. The father, mom, and son are Packer fanatics. It began long ago for the elder Breeden in Mount Washington where he grew up. Today, he owns a home in Green Bay, while Kentucky remains their full-time home—temporarily.

"Back in the earlier years, my favorites were Babe Parilli, Tobin Rote, and Tony Canadeo. Then Bart Starr and the '60s gang captured our hearts. With the Packers from a small town, everyone else was for the Giants or Browns, but I stood by my Packers," he acknowledges proudly.

Determined to make a visit to Green Bay to meet a few of his heroes, the first journey to Titletown for the Breedens came in 1982. They began and have continued to collect autographs in excess of 500 different Packers. They have become friends with many of the former Packer players and continue to make the nine hour commute to Green Bay from Kentucky during the season for selected games. If the Packers are in Indianapolis or Cincinnati, the Breedens are there.

When the Kentucky Packer contingent can't make it to Green Bay to enjoy the games in person, they can be found hosting Packer parties and watching the team on their satellite dish. A Packer club for displaced Wisconsinites and other Packer faithful congregates at Dutch's in Louis-ville.

Paul Hornung, the "Golden Boy" and former Packer great, does a show during the NFL season in Louisville. Last year the Breedens took in a show which Ray Nitschke was there as a guest. James Breeden was acknowledged on the show. Nitschke remembered and shared a special memory in which James was a part back in the early '70s.

"I had introduced James to my dog Butkus. (Dick Butkus was the great Chicago Bear linebacker who Ray played against.) James dropped by when we weren't home, but Butkus was on the front porch. He didn't know the dog was chained and he high-tailed it to the car!" he laughed.

Patrick has been a Packer fan since he was just a little boy. "Everything I got for Christmas had to have Green Bay Packers on it," he recalls. At times it took a leap of faith to hang in there till the skies cleared, but he has never wavered or compromised with his dedication to his team. "I took a lot of 'Packer abuse' in school growing up, but today it's different. Many have jumped on the bandwagon, and I think that's great!" says Patrick with a sweet, forgiving spirit.

His green blood is even thicker than perfume when it comes to his infatuation with the Packers. "My girlfriend told me she felt silly walking under my Packer umbrella with me. If I had to choose her or the Packers … well … she knows what I'd choose!" he laughs.

Patrick has in his possession something that is literally one in a million, a picture taken with former Packer Sterling Sharpe. Sharpe had a personal policy of not signing a lot of autographs while he played for the Packers from 1988-1994. Patrick Breeden was one of the lucky ones. It appears Packers and persistence go hand in hand.

"My Dad and I saw him in the Green Bay Packer parking lot and nobody was around. I walked over to him and asked if we could take a picture. He was great to us."

The *Green Bay Press-Gazette* has been delivered daily to the Breedens for years, but their greatest step of devotion to the Packers and the people of Wisconsin may have begun back in 1987.

"We purchased a home in Green Bay, which we really only have the opportunity to stay at when we're up for the games. We absolutely love the town, the people, and Wisconsin. In five years we hope to retire to Wisconsin and make it our permanent home," says James. With a proud southern drawl, the elder Breeden says, "We're going to be Wisconsinites!" Jim, you'll fit right in.

In Trout Creek, Michigan, where the excitement can be watching grass grow or cheesehead hats age, the Packers provide a bulk of entertainment for the neighbors to the east. Andrea Hull, a senior in Trout Creek, loves the Packers. Her senior class picture shows her tipping the brim of her Packer cap with a beautiful smile. She's wearing a dark green sweater.

"We listen to the games on the radio because we don't have a TV. When the Playoffs were on, we watched the game at our neighbors. We converted our neighbors to Packer fans!" she says.

So what is it about the Packers that broadens their appeal to not only the home folk, but the whole country, including Trout Creek? "One thing that we really appreciate about the Packers is the attitude of the team. Some of the other teams are arrogant and self-centered, but not Green Bay. They are regular people you can relate to."

Irwin Glassman, from Boulder, Colorado, is as great an example of how a romance can bloom when exposed to this fascinating team and the people who represent it. Glassman, 71, spent time as the director of technical operations for a large arsenal in Denver, destroying hazardous chemical waste. Being a Packer fan seems to have been nearly as dangerous. He went in head first. It started a long time ago.

"In August of 1937, my mother and father took me to Green Bay for a family wedding. We were living in New York City. A few of the Packers were there. I met Tiny Engebretsen and "Buckets" Goldenberg." Those gentle behemoths planted a seed that would begin to grow in the young 12-year old.

Although Glassman went back home to New York, he left his heart in Green Bay. "I returned home and a passionate love affair began with the Packers that has never abated for 59 years," says Glassman. "I used to walk to the corner of 42nd and Times Square to pick up a *Milwaukee Journal* so I could read about the Packers. My wife thought I would grow out of it, but then just got used to it," laughs Glassman.

The Packer management made it very easy to love the Packers for Irwin. The Glassmans married in 1956, and Irwin had a great idea for a honeymoon. "General Manager Vern Lewellyn sent me two tickets to attend the Green Bay opener." The Glassmans were two of 24,668 fans who were there. "We lost, 20-16," says Mr. Glassman as if it were just yesterday.

Other thrills involving the team have come to Glassman over the seasons. "Bart Starr spotted me at Stapleton Airport in Denver. I was wearing my Packer shirt. He had always answered my correspondence over the years."

A recurring Packer theme here, like with Patrick Breeden who met Sterling Sharpe, seems to reveal a loving responsiveness to their fans. So what makes the Packers so unique? Irwin Glassman, a fan for nearly 60 years, has his ideas.

"It all boils down to one sentence: They are a pro town with a college spirit! There is nothing like the town of Green Bay and the people. Even today in the greed engendered by free agency, the Packers come closest to achieving a team chemistry and bonding with the community that is fast disappearing from pro football. They are truly "the last of the Mohicans," says Glassman.

Barbara Glassman made her husband's week back in 1983. While working for a travel agency, she fooled Irwin into thinking she was taking him west. Little did he know he was coming east.

"Barbara said she wanted to surprise me. She told me to pack for San Diego. One thing puzzled me; she had packed some cold-weather clothes." A conversation on the plane prompted him to ask, "What's going on?" he recalls with a big grin. Needless to say he was thrilled to know he was on his way to the Packer-Viking game. Despite the fact the Packers lost the game played in Milwaukee, 20-17, in overtime, it's one of Irwin's great memories.

There's nothing unusual about being a Packer fan who is a charter member of the Packer Hall of Fame, own a brick in it, be a subscriber to the *Green Bay Press-Gazette* and *Packer Report*, and have seen about 40 Packer games in person. But to be from Texas, in the middle of Dallas Cowboy and Houston Oiler country, this does appear to be rather bold.

You've just met Keith Frentrup from deep in the heart of Austin, Texas, where he has been in love with the Packers since he was eight years old. Today, 45 years young, he's glued to ESPN and the Packer publications to find out what's the latest with his passion, the Green Bay Packers. Take it a step further, Keith is a candidate for President of the Green Bay Packermania Hall of Fame.

"I first got interested in the Packers when I saw some of the players on bubble gum cards in 1959 when I was nine." With a whimsical logic he says, "I liked the uniforms. I didn't know where Green Bay was until I looked it up," Keith noted jovially.

After 11 years of a long-distance love affair, he made a date for a face-to-face visit. In 1970, the pocket-sized 19-year-old got some end zone tickets to watch the Packers take on Buffalo in Lambeau for a pre-season contest. Frentrup remembers the time like it was yesterday. "My Mom knew it was a dream of mine to come to Green Bay. (Keith's Dad died in 1967.) She said it was okay for me to come." The Packers won, 34-0. He has seen 40 games since. Tampa, Kansas City, New Orleans, and Cincinnati are just a few of the places on the green-and-gold trail that Keith has been on with his out-of-town family.

Probably his greatest two friends since 1979 are his VCR and satellite dish, but he's gotten other help from his friends in Green Bay.

"I used to have a friend in Green Bay record the games and coach's show and mail them to me. I'd watch them six days later!"

Keith believes that the love affair between the Packers and their fans has a pretty simple explanation. "The Packers let you put a face inside the helmet instead of just a name and number on the jersey. Because of the size of the town and the way the Packers are so accessible at practices and stuff, you can talk to them one-on-one. Every time I'm in Green Bay around the Packers I feel like a kid at Disneyland."

Keith has gotten to know fellow Texans and Packer players Al Matthews, David Beverly, Mark Cannon, and Greg Koch. "I was at Matthews's and Koch's weddings. They were glad to see me there," he says proudly with a smile.

Keith has also gotten to know the Dickeys and the Coffmans, and he confesses that this special relationship makes it a little tougher to be tough on his family—the Packer players. "When you know some of the players personally, you realize that these people have feelings. They are more than just a number. You are less likely to yell at them or criticize them because they become family when you know them. They want to win the game more than you do."

Frentrup also knows first hand that things aren't like they are in Green Bay everywhere around the league. Keith offers this up close view of the Cowboys from his vantage point in Texas. "To me, the relationship between the Cowboys and their fans is artificial. The Cowboy fans are fair-weather fans. As long as they win, everything is great, but when they start losing, they won't support them. Between 1984 and 1991, the Cowboys only sold out a few games. It will happen when the Cowboys start losing again," Frentrup says boldly.

"The team practices, unlike the Packers, are closed to the public and the camp is 200 miles away. Even at the camp, it's tough to get autographs. There are only 30 teams in the NFL and the Cowboys are my 31st favorite," proclaims Frentrup.

Another great displaced Packer "snowbird" puts on the largest out-of-town Packer tailgate party every year in Tampa Bay, when the Packers play the Buccaneers.

Bob Goodwin, 70, from Beaver Dam, Wisconsin, who temporarily takes Florida residence during the winter, is the co-founder and co-ordinator of the Tampa Bay Packer Backer Club since 1977. It is the largest non-local fan club in the NFL. To date their largest attendance has been 5,600 enthusiastic Tampa Bay Packer Backers that attended the December 10, 1995 game in Tampa. The club has grown over the years through nothing more than word of mouth. Goodwin is also a Green Bay season ticket holder since 1959.

On October 23, 1977, 105 Packer fans showed up for the first Tampa Bay Packer Backer Party. The first year consisted of a brunch at the Admiral Benbow Hotel. Goodwin reminisces, "Ray Scott, was doing radio for the Buccaneers and agreed to come over and be our Master of Ceremonies. The following year membership rose to 165 with a Saturday evening sit-down dinner at the Holiday Inn. Coach Bart Starr and wife Cherry stopped in and extended their best wishes to the fans.

On October 12, 1980, the club had their very first tailgate party. Brats, liquid refreshments, and fellowship took place in the parking lot south of the stadium. They knew they had found the right combination as membership exploded to 345 that year.

All has not gone smooth over the years for the club. There have been two strike years which have interrupted the festivities. In 1987 the club had made preparations for the game not knowing if the strike would be settled. The only game canceled that year was the one in Tampa. "All the monies had to be refunded," remembers Goodwin. In 1983, a Monday night game presented lighting problems. "We had people shining their car lights. It was a little difficult, but we still had fun," said Goodwin.

By 1995, the Tampa Bay Packer Backer Club, by word of mouth only, had grown to 5,600 members! Participation from 24 states shows conclusively that the tremendous Packer allegiance has absolutely no boundaries.

Currently the night before the game, the club has sponsored the "Packer Polka Party," which includes The Frankie Yankovic Band from Ohio and Gordon Hartman's Polka Band from Madison, Wisconsin.

In 1995, Johnsonville Foods brought their 72-foot "big taste grill" mounted on a semi to grill and cook their tasty Wisconsin bratwurst. (Are there any other kinds?) Cool refreshments flowed. If the game can't be in Green Bay, this sounds like the second greatest place for a Packer party to be.

Throughout the years, you could have run into Boyd Dowler, Bob Long, Ray Nitschke, Dave "Hog" Hanner, and other former Packers at one of the group's gatherings. Goodwin is quick to thank Leonard Liebman, Jerry "Mouse" Rauwald, Ted Lauck, Tom Lom, Bob Clancy, Ron Peura, "Green Bay Ray" Blake, and countless others who have helped build the Tampa Bay Packer Backer Club. Bob was asked, "Are the Packer fans the greatest?"

"There is nothing even close! Being a Packer fan is something special. There is nothing comparable—anywhere."

When you have developed a club of 5,600 Packer fans, you can make such strong statements. But, Bob, why are they the greatest?

"I believe it's because you don't have the greedy owners. With the team community owned, the fans feel the Packers are truly 'their' team."

Amen.

Thirteen

"I Was There; I Ain't Snowin' You!"

God has a great sense of humor. In the history of the National Football League, He's allowed Mother Nature to bring to Green Bay a couple of memorable, weather-related games. Two come to mind that have gone down in history. One, an NFL title game with a wind chill of 50 degrees below zero; the other, a December blizzard.

Because of the uncertainty of the weather in Green Bay, fans have been treated to more than just these two, but they show that neither wind, rain, or snow can keep Packer fans away from Lambeau Field.

On New Years Eve, 1967, the Packers hosted the Dallas Cowboys in the historic battle known today as the "Ice Bowl". Kickoff temperature was 15 degrees below zero with a wind chill factor of minus 49.

From this clash, John Facenda, the unmistakable, resonant voice of NFL Films for so many years, coined his classic phrase, "the frozen tundra of Lambeau Field." Despite the threat of frostbite, extreme discomfort, and other misery, thousands of Packers fans filled Lambeau Field to support the green-and-gold. Hundred of thousands of people said they were there, but only about 50,861 actually were.

Marion Rife, of Kaukauna, Wisconsin, was one of those who braved the bitter cold. She went with her brother David. How did they survive? "We wore layers of clothes, plus had sleeping blankets around us. We were concerned that with everyone bundled up, everyone would take up a seat and a half!" she said. "Actually, the game was with such a fever pitch, we really didn't get that cold. We were up in the wind too," she pointed out.

Apparently, they don't make fans in Dallas like they do in Green Bay. Marion recounts that a Packer fan she knew told this gem. He had gone to the concession area where he saw this Texan with a Stetson Hat, Cowboy boots, and a thin Denim jacket. Very naively, the man made the comment, "Man, it sure is co-o-o-ld up here!" To make the guy feel just a little bit colder, and not missing an opportunity to have fun with a Cowboy fan, the Wisconsinite said, "This is nothing, you should be here in the dead of winter!"

To give you a little better idea of just how cold it was, all liquid refreshments were kept in ovens to keep them in their liquid state. The band also was prohibited from playing because all the brass instruments stuck to the lips of the musicians.

Bob Skoronski, a Packer who played in the game, said, "Ironically, there were more Packers with frostbite than Dallas Cowboys." Tough to figure that one out other than maybe with Coach Lombardi looming the sidelines, the guys may have been a little cautious about standing by the heater."

The Ice Bowl had one of the most dramatic game finishes of all time. With 16 seconds left, Bart Starr snuck into the end zone behind Jerry Kramer's block for a 21-17 Packer victory. The win propelled them into the second Super Bowl, where the Packers beat down the Oakland Raiders, 33-14.

Nearly 18 years after the "Ice Bowl", my wife and I had the joy of being caught in the middle of the other Packer classic called the "Snow Bowl". It has gone down in the record books as having had the greatest accumulation of snow during a game. This was nearly one foot, and that didn't include the foot that had fallen before the game.

Until 1983 when I married Kim, she didn't know the Packers existed. She grew up in Iowa where professional teams are rarer than two dollar bills. Matter of fact, there aren't any professional teams there at all. If you aren't a Cyclone or Hawkeye fan, you're out of luck.

In the early '80s, Kim used to be content to spend her time from noon to 3:00 p.m. each Packer game day to cross-stitch, do laundry, or shop. Things have gradually, yet drastically changed over the years with my present day Packer monster. These present day Lambeau Leapers have a way of wearing a person down, then pulling you in. She caught Packermania in 1985. This was when being poked in the eye with a sharp stick was nearly as enjoyable as watching the Ditka-laced Bears pummel the Packers twice annually.

In September, while the weather was still beautiful she asked me, "Can you get us some tickets to a Packer game sometime?" I nearly fell off my rocker. This was the woman who told me she had never heard of the Packers until she came here and was as committed to the Packers as a kamikaze pilot on his seventh mission.

At the time, I was a radio personality in the Fox River Valley, and quite often folks would call in with a ticket or two to unload. The thing that is very unique—and remains to this day—is that the majority of people who sell their Packer tickets will do so at nearly face value. Their is very little "gouging" that goes on when unloading the tickets.

Sure enough, just as I had hoped, someone called the station to sell two tickets. I proudly brought the trophies to my queen. We had two great seats for the December 1 game in Green Bay versus the Tampa Bay Buccaneers.

The night before the game, the weatherman was calling for snow—lots of it. Like a couple feet. He insinuated that it might be a good idea for those attending the Packer game the next day to make a dash to get to town early, like the night before.

With the thought of a wonderful night of dining and quiet time, I called the Midway Motor Lodge across the street from Lambeau Field. It really was amazing that somehow we were able to get a room the night before a Packer game.

We arrived in Green Bay late Saturday afternoon, the day before the game. By 11:00 p.m. no sign of snow. When I awoke at about 4:00 a.m., it was a different story. A few hours earlier I could see our pretty metallic blue Audi in the parking lot. Now there was this huge drift becoming larger, covering the car by the second.

We ate breakfast the next morning then got dressed. We covered ourselves in layers of clothing. I had a good pair of coveralls while Kim had a nice big coat and a couple pair of pants. We both had those groovy looking moon boots on. We made a twenty minute trek through the deep snow drifts to the stadium. It should have taken only five minutes.

On this day, the game was secondary.

Ken Ruettgers told me, "If there was a game I thought should have been canceled, it was that one." That should tell you something.

But my sweetie got her wish. It was still snowing like crazy. About a foot had fallen up to this point.

Normally, Lambeau Filed would be jammed with fans. On this day, a little over 19,000 were there. Most of the diehards literally couldn't make it. The TV people were telling everyone to stay home. We were two of the lucky ones—I think.

As I took my seat beforehand in the blizzard, I asked myself a couple questions: How am I going to see the game? What am I doing here? The most important question, with no answer, flashed before my half-a-mind. Bundled up like a little boy to go out and make a snowman, I thought, What am I going to do if I have to go to the bathroom?

Liquid refreshments were out for me.

The game began.

Trying to keep my glasses clean from the snow was about as frustrating as trying to blow out a light bulb. I needed eye glass windshield wipers.

We were perched about half way up the stands in the end zone. We could have sat anywhere we wanted. The place was only about one third full. I squinted to see moving figures of green and gold. On the other side were some men in snow white and burnt orange. I assumed they were the Tampa Bay players.

I had a radio with headphones listening to Packer broadcasters Jim Irwin and Max McGee. At least I knew a little of what was going on. Kim couldn't see anything, but was at least staying dry. She put this funky plastic stuff over her clothing. Funny looking, but effective. That day making a fashion statement wasn't important.

Three hours later, we were headed out of the stadium after a Packer win, 27-0.

I will never forget two things about the game. One was Lynn Dickey's success throwing to James Lofton, and the other was seeing Steve Young, the young Tampa Bay quarterback, pulling snow out of his face mask. Packer lineman Alphonso Carreker had sacked him and pushed his head into the snow!

We were trapped in Green Bay for an extra day. A hundred-dollar weekend had turned into about three bills. After we got home and dug out, I remember Kim saying, "I am not going to go to another game again unless it's in September!" If we do, I'm sure it will snow.

December 31, 1967—the "Ice Bowl". December 1, 1985, this game was known as the "Snow Bowl". Many say they were there, but for the latter, "We *were* there; I ain't snowin' you!"

MARK INGRAM spent only one season in Green Bay, but his contribution to the Packers offense was more than adequate.

DARIUS HOLLAND played sparingly in his initial season with the Packers, but big things are expected of him in the future.

Fourteen

Ken Ruettgers: Role Model

We were rolling down the Lombardi Avenue access road in Ken's big, white Suburban of salvation, heading to have lunch at Red Lobster. As it turned out, it's wasn't just a lunch; it was a banquet!

Ken was in a great mood, although he was going on just a few winks of sleep; I assumed he was running on fumes, the sweet smell of victory the night before over the Bears. The Packers' charter flight hadn't returned to Green Bay until 1:30 a.m.. A nap was probably in the offing, but he loves to eat. So do I, and that's where we were going.

The important thing was that the Packers had shellacked the Bears, 33-6, on Halloween night in Chicago. "ABC Monday Night Football" had brought the contest to homes throughout the country. It was cold, windy, and rainy. Not a night fit for man nor beast, except when the men are beasts and the game is football.

"Man, it was cold last night. The cold air pasted our wet uniforms to us," Ken said with a twinge of a shiver in his voice.

As we cruised, I couldn't help but tease Ken about the Packers' throwback uniforms they'd worn in the game. To mark the league's 75th season, NFL team's wore old uniforms for some games. The Packers chose the uniforms from the 1930s and 1940s. They included blue and gold jerseys, beige pants, and yellow helmets. The helmets made each Packer head look like a giant yellow gum drop.

During the nationally televised game Ruettgers had provided a little Halloween present for the national audience. Late in the game with Packers safely ahead, the audience saw jack-o-lantern decals on the back of his helmet. He expected a fine from the league for his bit of fun. But none was levied. Even the league office must have thought it was cute.

"My brother put me up to it," said the big tackle. "He sent them to me. The fact that the game was in the bag made me a little bolder."

Just five hours earlier at 6:50 a.m., Ken had walked into the studio in a beautiful, long-sleeved, dark brown sweater. He set down the treats and gave me a hug. I could tell he was relieved the Packers were back in the win column. He was probably happy to be warm, too. And now we were having fun laughing and joking as we headed to Red Lobster.

Within minutes as we were being taken to a table by a waitress, a guy spotted Kenny and yelled playfully, "Ken, have you thawed out from last night yet?"

"Yeah, I'll be okay," Ruettgers laughed.

"Good game, Ken."

"Thanks."

We ordered. Ken had blackened salmon; I had the perch. We had all the trimmings—crab legs, soups, those incredible butter buns, water, soda, coffee, cake, ice cream—the works. Ken dunked his crab legs into the butter while eating his salad—dry. (I think it's kind of like the person who orders a Big Mac, fries, and then a Diet Coke.)

Two hours after we began eating, our waitress presented us with the check. "You can pay me when you want," she said gleefully as she set it on the table.

I took it, put it down in front of me, and reached for my wallet.

"No, please," Ken insisted. He pulled out his billfold. It looked about fifteen years old, was beat up, and faded. A million little pieces of paper were hanging out of it. He perused it's contents and coolly pulled out a fifty dollar bill and a couple ones. Ken threw a ten on the table for a tip as we left.

It was a minor miracle we were able to leave there under our own power. What we'd experienced was what they must mean when they talk about a "power lunch."

One of the great visions and calls from the Lord that Ken has fulfilled was writing a book called, *Home Field Advantage: A Dad's Guide to the Power of Role Modeling*. It's a fantastic book. One day when I was at Ken's place, I watched the book come to life right before my eyes, nine months before it even came out!

I'll never forget the day I met his wife Sheryl. She probably won't either. I'd only talked to her on the phone up until that time. What a great person! She had this incredible energy and love for life. Bouncy, bubbly. I wasn't disappointed when I met her.

Ken had asked me one morning after a show in 1994 to go to breakfast, and this was my opportunity to meet Sheryl and see some things that were so precious. Within minutes of the show, Ken was leading me into his home, and we walked down the hall to some stairs.

Coming down the steps was this cute, petite brunette, holding a hammer in one hand and a dirty diaper in the other. "Kenny, why didn't you tell me you were bringing company home?" she said.

"It's just Steve," said Ken with his arm around me. Ken kissed her. I felt like part of the family. I walked over to the smiling lady.

"Sheryl, it's good to finally see you." I gave her a hug.

"You, too."

Ken had bragged about her so much. It didn't take long for me to see why. What a glorious couple they make!

On the way down the hall, we popped into Ken's office. On his desk was the computer he was using to write his book. Taped on the side of it was Jack Del Rio's phone number. He and Del Rio played in college together at the University of Southern California. On the fireplace mantle was his beat-up USC football helmet, next to a few of the Packer game footballs awarded to him by his teammates.

"September 15, 1985. I remember that game," I said as I looked at one of the footballs. "It was against the Giants in Green Bay." That was over 10 years ago, but I remembered it like it was yesterday. I watched it at my brother Dale's.

Then on the wall I saw a picture of Ken and Brian Noble from a Coke commercial. They looked like they had just played a hard-fought game. Sweaty, muddy; you could practically smell them.

"Naw, it's fake!" admitted Ruettgers. "It's all artificial. The picture was taken in a photo studio. They sprayed water on our faces to make us look like we were sweating. They applied the mud to our uniforms."

It sure looked legit to me.

Two little girls came running down the steps; cute little blondes named Katherine and Susan; ages two and four. They gave their hunched over dad a kiss. You didn't need to be very observant to realize that this household of five is held together with love.

It was time to take son Matt to school. "Matt, let's go!" yelled the man of the house.

We hopped into the Ruettgersmobile, and off we went. It was a sunny, pretty, colorful fall morning. Five minutes later, we picked up the neighbor boy, a classmate of Matt's.

"Good morning Mr. Ruettgers," the little tyke said happily as he climbed into the back seat next to Matt. He and Matt chatted Ken and I continued to solve the world's problems.

We pulled into the school's driveway. The neighbor boy jumped out and said gratefully, "Thanks Mr. Ruettgers."

Matt lunged between the bucket seats, directly behind his father, and planted a kiss on his dad's cheek. Two seconds later he vanished.

"It's a rush to see your boy running off to school," the proud dad proclaimed.

Ken was certainly Matt's hero, and he should be. My dad is to me.

Before we left the parking lot of the elementary school, my mind drifted back to fifth grade, 25 years ago. I read a book about another one of my heroes, Bart Starr. He used to pick up the neighbor kids in Green Bay and take them to McDonald's for all the burgers, fries, and cokes they could eat and drink.

It didn't click till months later that I had witnessed in 30 minutes that day what Ken Ruettgers would talk about so sensitively and eloquently in his book. In the book, Ken talks family, writes family, and lives family, all in the spirit of Jesus Christ. I saw it in a powerful way that morning.

From the school, we breezed down some side streets to Country Kitchen for breakfast. The big man had some egg whites and something else healthy, like dry toast, while I had the whole package—sausages, pancakes, eggs. You name it, I had it and didn't feel the least bit guilty, but got a case of heartburn later. A cone from the Dairy Queen helped to soothe it.

During our meal that morning, I remember sharing a vision with Ken about a personal development seminar I was writing at the time called *Seven Steps From Your Dreams to Your Destiny*. I asked Ken if he would write a couple quotes of endorsement for me. He said he'd be happy to. He wrote: "Steve Rose has had an immeasurable effect on myself and my team-mates. His infectious, optimistic perspectives give you a new lease on life." Today, like many of my other dreams, I present this seminar to audiences of all sizes.

We jumped into Ken's truck for the five-minute ride to the studio, where I'd left my car. Ken dropped me off and sped across the street to work in his office: Lambeau Field and the Packer practice facilities.

The next week on the "Timeout" program Ken gave an indication of what a truly wonderful man he is and why his family is crazy about him. I believe it will give you a good picture of Ken Ruettgers more than the man who has protected the blind side of numerous Packer quarterbacks, since 1985. He also provides loving protection at home.

I started the show asking, "What did you do last night, my friend."

"I had a date," he said.

"Really, where'd you and Sheryl go?"

"I didn't take my wife," he said seriously.

I coughed and just about spit coffee all over Ken. His answer caught me just a wee bit off guard. Rarely am I left without words, but this time I sat perfectly still. Ken had just said he had a date, but not with his wife. Okay. I wasn't sure how to continue, and then my trusted friend bailed me out.

"I went out with my daughter Katherine," said Ruettgers. I breathed a sigh of relief. "She polished her nails, curled her hair, and put on a cute little outfit. We went out to eat and to a movie. It was a real opportunity to spend some quality time with her."

Picture this huge, handsome man holding the hand of his petite little blonde that's cuter than a kitten. It's something he does often. That's the Ken Ruettgers I have gotten to know.

Besides Red Lobster, Ken and I love eating ice cream. The big man, his son Matthew, and I were in Appleton after the 1995 season, and the subject came up.

"Matt, maybe Steve will treat us at the Diary Queen."

"You got it, gentlemen!" I was easy. For Ken and me, going to the Dairy Queen is like a Packer fan going to Lambeau Field. We found one on Richmond Street.

We stood at the counter.

"What do you want?" Ken asked.

"I gotta have a Butterfinger Blizzard, what else?" I said.

It was Ken's turn to order. "Give me one of those," Ken said pointing at a gooey Peanut Buster Parfait a young lady was holding.

Behind me, over my left shoulder, I spotted three teenagers who recognized Ken. I backed up and whispered to them, "It's Brett Favre doing his Ken Ruettgers imitation!"

They laughed.

Ken turned around.

"Guys, meet Ken Ruettgers."

They froze in the presence of the Packer lineman.

"What's your name," Ken asked one of the boys. Ruettgers has an incredible way of making people feel special when he meets them.

"What school do you guys go to?" I asked.

"Appleton North."

Playfully, I said to Ken, "It's important for you to have some ice cream to keep your goal line muscle strong, right?" His goal line muscle is his waist! "You can't be too light when you got Charles Haley of the Dallas Cowboys pushing you around!"

"Yeah, this is training!" he laughed.

We all chuckled as Ken slapped a high five on me. Those kids were eating this up. So was I.

I had Ken sign a copy of his book for them. The kids left with the looks of giddy third-graders. You just never know who you will run into at the Dairy Queen.

We finished up our treats and our conversation.

"I gotta get Matthew home to bed."

"Was good to see you, brother. Say hi to Sheryl," I concluded.

"You take care, bud," he said as he stuck out his incredibly large hand. Then he and Matthew vanished out the side door.

The day I met Ken Ruettgers, admittedly, I was awed by his size and physique. I have to admit that it would have been easy for me to have bought the book after seeing only the cover. And I'm not talking about *Home Field Advantage*. With each opportunity to be with Ken, he blesses me.

On April 29, 1996, Ken was invited to speak in Fond du Lac at the Moraine Park Technical Institute. Fond du Lac is one of the prettiest towns in all of the state of Wisconsin. It's about an hour and a half south of Green Bay, right at the top of beautiful Lake Winnebago. (Top of the lake because water flows from top to bottom, and although Fond du Lac is at the south end of the lake, the water flows north from there.)

We arrived at the Moraine Park Technical Institute, and Ken, Sheryl, and I came in together. Ken did a quick interview, and then we went in and sat down at a table near the podium where Ken would address the crowd of nearly 500.

"Ken, let me pray for you quickly," I said as he was being introduced.

"Okay."

I reached over to my left and grabbed his arm and prayed that God would give him the strength and boldness to share the message in his heart.

"Thanks," he whispered as I finished. Right at that moment, the speaker said, "Ladies and gentlemen, please give a warm welcome to Mr. Ken Ruettgers." I felt like I was on the top of the world. Here was my friend speaking near my hometown. I was so proud of him.

Ken—and his message for the Family Resource Center—was anointed. He talked of having taken Matthew to the Super Bowl, the bonding with his daughters, the importance of having a good wife like Sheryl. It was very enjoyable.

Mom and a bunch of the family were there. Mom and Ken had a picture taken together.

As the night came to an end, Ken and I walked in the parking lot. It was a miserable evening as a wet, painful sleet pelted our faces. Ken held a group of papers over his head. He gave me a ride to my car.

"Bob McGinn, from the *Milwaukee Journal Sentinel*, said he talked with you about your book and Robert Brooks is pretty excited about it too," he told me.

He drove me to my car in the corner of the dark parking lot.

"Ken, I'm so proud of you. You did a great job tonight" I told him.

"Thanks, call me soon," he said as I slammed the door and lunged for my LeBaron. And then something very spiritual happened.

Ken and Sheryl pulled out of the driveway and took a left. I took a right. About 20 minutes later, I approached Oshkosh, on highway 41. My windshield wipers were in overdrive pushing and smearing the wet, white, heavy slush off my windshield. Right then, I recognized the Ruettgers passing me on my left. Must be great to have four-wheel drive at a time like this, I thought. I stayed right behind them. I was following them like a little duck behind the mother. As we went over the Butte des Morts Bridge, I noticed Ken swerving, pulling back to the left about three feet, and back onto the four-lane highway, so did I. We had just about driven into the ditch together!

Just seconds afterward, the message came to me. "Be careful about who you are following. If they run off the road of life and into the ditch, you will too. Keep your eyes on Jesus. He'll always keep you on the right road, but you have to follow Him."

Now Ken hadn't intentionally tried to lead me into the ditch. Matter-of-fact, he didn't even know I was following him. Ask yourself this question. As role models, are we being careful not to run them into the ditch with us? Who are the ones following us?

It was a powerful revelation. The great news is Ken Ruettgers is well aware that he is a role model and has done his share to lead. I love Ken dearly, as I do my brothers. He has shown me that if you want to build other people up, then put them on your shoulders. Ken has been impressive with his play on the field for the Packers, but his real ministry is eternal and maybe someday will be a full-time ministry, one of sharing with others how they also can keep the *Home Field Advantage.*

Fifteen

The Greatest
Leap of Faith Yet

Packer star quarterback Brett Favre has thrown a few bombs in Green Bay over the last few years, but none like the one he dropped on May 14, 1996.

It was a cool, dreary afternoon. I was gazing out the window of my office. Off to the side, I heard this bit of bright news from the USA Radio Network. "And in sports, the Green Bay Packers have announced quarterback Brett Favre has voluntarily entered the NFL substance abuse program."

Good news? That's right. Few understand that when you hit the bottom, it can be time for celebration. Really, it's the only place you can begin to bounce up again. A big part of beating any addiction problem is acknowledging that you have one, and Brett Favre did that. It's a decision that very well may have saved his life.

It seems like just yesterday—actually over five years ago—when I had to make the same decision myself. For me it was alcoholism. I can confirm with Brett—and millions of other addicts—that it's not a really great moment when you admit you have a problem with alcohol and drugs. Many think *denile* is a river in Egypt, when *denial* is what seals an addict into bondage.

It's no picnic making this declaration to your family, friends, and the world. Matter-of-fact, the thought of an all-day root canal at the dentist, being locked in a cell with a Doberman pincer, or having toothpicks driven under your fingernails is much more appealing. However, the admission of a problem and providing the surrender necessary to deal with it is the doorway to hope, help, and miracles.

So while others around Packerdom may have been feeling pretty bummed out about the news, I was thrilled knowing what could be ahead for Favre, if he can yield to God's chastening in his life to find unadulterated recovery. That means total abstinence from all drugs, alcohol, painkillers—everything.

Favre knows his battle is against something more dangerous than the Dallas Cowboys defensive line.

Favre acknowledged his long road ahead. "It's not an easy thing, but hopefully I can help other people because it's something very serious, and it's something I have to take care of." Visibly shaken, he continued saying, "With the support of Coach Holmgren and Ron Wolf (Packer general manager), the NFL, family, friends, and you guys (the media), I'll get through this."

So what went through your mind as you heard the news? Did you feel sorry for him or did you want to ridicule him? Jesus said, "He who is without sin, cast the first stone." If you live in a glass house like most people, stay out of the gravel pit. The passage that bonded Ken Ruettgers and myself was the verse about logs and specks. Again, Jesus said, "Don't tell your brother about the sliver in his eye when you have a log in yours." (Matthew 7:3) Whoa!

It's understandable, yet somewhat unacceptable for many people to feel that Brett Favre has lost his opportunity to be a role model. Nothing could be further from the truth. It is at this point that he has the greatest chance. What would have happened if Brett would have been intoxicated on painkillers and seriously injured or even killed someone on a Green Bay street? Then how would you have felt? With his confession, he's on the road to incredible spiritual and personal growth.

Again, we need to look in our own mirror. Cut Brett some slack, if you haven't already. You see, God tells us that we all have things we are using to kill our pain.

One of the greatest gifts, besides love, that God has given us is the gift of choice. It very well may have been the greatest chance He took when He created us. He could have made us all automatons, but that would have taken the fun out of life for all of us. I pray that you will make good choices, including those God would want you to make today.

A couple more things about Favre. I have an incredible feeling that he will make a tremendously positive impact on people from having made this humble decision. God has promised to bless him. Scripture states: "The exalted will be humbled, and the humbled will be exalted." Watch what happens with Favre. It's going to be another miracle in the long line of miracles that have graced the Packers over the years.

During Favre's first news conference after completing his treatment for substance abuse, he said: "First of all, I want to thank the fans for all their support." He'd already thanked God.

As a side note, take in this God-incidence. Almost one year before the day Brett made his announcement that he was entering a rehab facility, Dwight "Doc" Gooden, the star major league pitcher, was suspended for drug use. Gooden subsequently entered a rehab center and got himself cleaned out—body and soul. On the very same day that Brett made his announcement to do the same, Gooden pitched a 2-0 no-hitter for the New York Yankees! Could this be a sign from God? A God-incidence? Or was it merely a co-incidence? It will be exciting to see what will happen with Brett Favre as he continues to recover.

Jesus said in Matthew 5:14-16: "You are the light of the world. A city set on a hill cannot be hid. Nor do men light a lamp and put it under a bushel, but on a stand, and it gives light to all in the house. Let your light so shine before men, that they may see your good works and give glory to your Father who is in heaven."

None know this better than Reggie White, Ken Ruettgers, Robert Brooks, Adam Timmerman, and so many more Green Bay Packers. They have made the commitment to God, and they fear not to show it after every game as they kneel in the center of the field to thank Him in prayer. Note that they do this no matter who wins the game, and they will continue to praise God whether they win the Super Bowl or stumble along the way. Theirs is a giant leap of faith.

Can we as fans do no less?

That is a question that each of us must ask ourselves and pray that we come up with the right answer.

Thank you for taking the time to read this book. I pray that I have been able to show you that God's hand just might be behind this team, the Green Bay Packers. And if I've come up short on that score, well, may God's blessings be upon you and yours for all time anyway.

Acknowledgments

First of all, thanks to two of the most special people on this earth, my mom and dad, Jean and David Rose. I couldn't have picked a better set of parents. Matter-of-fact, I didn't—God did. Dad, thanks for being my role model of honesty and integrity long enough for me to catch it. And Mom, you are "walking love" wherever you go. I learn so much about love from you everyday. I love you both. Thanks for making it possible for me to be here!

To Gloria, Jim, Gary, Dan, Dale, and Sandi and Shari, well, you guys know this book is for you, too. Special thanks to my publicist-cheerleader since my birth, my brother Gary. I will never be able to measure what his encouragement has done for me.

Thanks to Vic Eliason and my family at the VCY America Christian Radio Network. You guys are a real testimony of God's faithfulness. Thanks for your support and making it possible for me to write this. Does God work in magnificent ways, or what?

Thanks to everyone at WORQ, 90.1 FM, in Green Bay. I speak of Chuck Towns, Kid Raider, Scotty Grathen, Ron and Karen Grosse, Lee and Joyce Dudek, and Dr. Ray Roddin. You're great!

A big thanks to my friend Ken Ruettgers, who is probably more responsible than anyone, after the Lord, for this book. Ken, you are truly one of the most incredible people I know. Thanks for supporting my message and all the things you've taught me about discipline and what it takes to win. I love you and Sheryl as I do my family.

Jim Zielinski (Felix Templeton to the nostalgia radio folks in Fond du Lac), you're one in a million. Thanks for the phone call at 10:40am on December 22, 1995, to suggest I write this book. Who would have thought back in those early days at WFON that we'd be writing books? Thanks for being my friend.

To my Senior Pastor, Bill Myers, and the loving family at First

Assembly in Appleton, Wisconsin, God's up to something big with y'all! Pastor, the incredible sacrifice you make everyday for the body of Christ is humbling to a baby Christian like me. I'll always follow you, as I see *Christ* leading *you*. My prayer was to put a piece of all of you in this book. Vicki Schroeder, thanks for all your enthusiasm; I caught it!

Additional thanks to Pastor Balken at Lighthouse Christian Church in Fond du Lac. (You guys were praying for me behind my back weren't you?)

I would really be remiss if I didn't thank *everyone* from back home in Campbellsport, Eden, and Fond du Lac, Wisconsin. A big thank you to Jerry Ninneman at the *Campbellsport News*, who helped to push me to where I am today. Jerry, when I figure out just exactly where I am, I'll let you know!

My sincere heartfelt gratitude goes to Angel Press of WI, who made it possible for this book to be in your hands. Apparently nobody told them you're not supposed to take a chance on one of those "first time" authors. They knew what God was telling them to do and unwaveringly did it. God bless you guys.

To my editor, Packer historian and bestselling author, Larry Names, you deserve a medal of honor for doing such a great job with the dangling participles and adverbs in this book. And Larry, that "Cub fanaticism" thing you suffer from, it is curable. There is some sort of counseling, I'm sure, for you and my dad, who suffers from a similar ailment. Seriously, thanks for your patience with me and allowing me to dream big dreams.

And to one who has watched many of the miracles, before there were any, Brad Vivoda, thanks for being there through it all. We did it Buddy!

Mike Utech, thanks for believing in me and being there to help when everyone else required something in return. Your servant's heart is like none I have ever known. Enjoy the voyage. You deserve to be along.

Brian Toelle, you are more of an answer to prayer than you will ever know. I accept the responsibility and the duties God has called us to accomplish in His name. When God had "winners" in mind, He created you. I've seen your tomorrow. It's unbelievable!

To my little brother, Robert Brooks, thanks for trusting me. Every time I look at you I will always ask, "With as tiny as you are, why don't you break apart like a pretzel when those thugs slam into you on Lambeau Field?"

Thanks to Packer President Bob Harlan. Bob, it's no secret why the Packers are winners—because you are! Lee Remmel and Linda McCrossin, thanks.

To Peter King, Greta Van Susteren, Bob McGinn, and Michael Bauman, thanks for giving me one of your most valuable assets—your time—to make this dream a reality. I hope to take your generosity and example of helping others, like me, forward.

Lastly, to my friend, Howie, see you in heaven where we'll watch the Packers every Sunday—forever.

About the Author

Steve Rose is a native of Eden, Wisconsin. He has worked in radio most of his adult life. He and wife Kim live in Neenah, Wisconsin. This is his first book.

Rose is also an accomplished inspirational speaker with a wide audience. John Gillespie of Rawhide Boys Ranch near New London, Wisconsin says Rose's seminar, *7 STEPS FROM YOUR DREAMS TO YOUR DESTINY*, "explains in simple, clear terms the attitude needed to succeed at anything in life. Steve's presentation was the most practical, down-to-earth presentation on goal-setting I have ever heard."